Latinas in
AVIATION

Stories of passion, power, and breaking into the aviation industry

Parks & Recreation
M-N C P P C

live more, play more
pgparks.com

MARYLAND EDITION
College Park Aviation Museum
Field of Firsts Foundation, Inc.

Latinas in AVIATION
MARYLAND EDITION

This book is a compilation of stories from numerous people who have each contributed a chapter and is designed to provide inspiration to our readers.

It is sold with the understanding that the publisher and the individual authors are not engaged in the rendering of psychological, legal, accounting or other professional advice. The content and views in each chapter are the sole expression and opinion of its author and not necessarily the views of Fig Factor Media, LLC.

For more information visit:

Fig Factor Media, LLC | www.figfactormedia.com
Cover Design by Juan Pablo Ruiz
Layout by LDG Juan Manuel Serna Rosales

Printed in the United States of America

ISBN: 978-1-957058-78-8
Library of Congress Number: 2022916265

This book is dedicated to everyone who ever doubted their ability to reach their dreams. *¡Sí se puede!*

Table of Contents:

Acknowledgements 6

Preface by Bill Fernandez 8

Introduction 12

AUTHOR CHAPTERS 16

FRANCES M. VELAZQUEZ
Whatever the Weather 17

ERYKA SILVA
Never Giving Up the Dream 27

LEENA CARLVALHO
Sprouting a Career in Real Estate 37

KEANNE VALLEJO-HUERTAS
Standing My Ground 45

ELIANA ROTHWELL
Reaching Out to My Dreams 55

RAQUEL VILLAGOMEZ
Adventure Turns Into Passion 65

LUCIA MENCIA
Reaching Out to My Dreams 75

NORMABAT-SHEVA ORONA-SAMMS
More Than My Resumé 85

MELISSA TORRES
Flying like George 95

ELIZABETH GARCIA CORVINGTON
Flying into a Career at Smithsonian Air and Space Museum 105

KAREN PEREZ
Sometimes it is Rocket Science 113

BRENDA GARCIA
All it Takes is a Moment 123

LUZ BEATTIE
One Small Magazine Leads to a Lifetime of Experiences 131

LOUISA OCASIO
A Latina in Control 141

About the Authors 151

ACKNOWLEDGEMENTS

There is an endless list of acknowledgements so I will try to be brief.

First, I would like to thank my family—Haydee, Sofia and Henry—for all the support they have given me as we transitioned from California to a new community in Maryland during a historic moment in the world.

I would like to thank my mom, the hardest working Latina I know. Thank you for all you have sacrificed for our family.

I wish to thank Jackie Ruiz and all the Latinas who made the first ever Latinas in Aviation Global Festival a huge success and inspiration to dive into a second volume.

Thank you to Jamie Jones and the entire College Park Aviation Museum team for all your hard work and dedication as we have worked on this project.

Thank you to the College Park Airport staff for all your support.

I wish to thank Omar Eaton-Martinez, Chris Fanning and all my Natural and Historic Resources Division colleagues for all their support and their community work.

I want to thank the Maryland National Capital Park and Planning Commission, Department of Parks and Recreation for preserving the treasure that is College Park Airport and supporting our amazing College Park Aviation Museum facility.

Thank you to the Field of Firsts Foundation Inc. for supporting this project and the vision of College Park Aviation Museum. Your support is greatly appreciated.

I want to thank all the community members that I have worked with over the years that impacted my work. I look at my work through the lens of you. It is the community that motivates me to do better and to always remember that my museum work is for the benefit of our community. Thank you!

-Kevin Cabrera

PREFACE

In 2017, I had the opportunity to hear former Federal Aviation Administration (FAA) Administrator Michael Huerta speak at our National Hispanic Coalition of Federal Aviation Employees (NHCFAE) Annual Training Conference. He was telling a story of an interview he had with reporters, how as a young Mexican boy in Southern California he would ride his bike by a local general aviation airport and spend hours watching the planes fly in and out of the airport.

A reporter asked him if that is what inspired him in a career in aviation. Mr. Huerta responded "No." He said, "You have to understand, where I grew up, neither of my parents spoke English until they started school. My dad didn't finish high school. What I was watching to me was something completely out of reach! It was something I couldn't fathom would ever be a part of my life and my career." He went on to say, "This is what all of us need to do. How many kids out there in the community that might be intrigued by a career in aviation, but might think it is completely out of reach?" Administrator Huerta challenged us that day to help young people find a rewarding career in aviation.

I was also a young boy from Southern California, who couldn't have "fathomed" a career in aviation. I joined the Air Force at 17, after losing a friend to what we now call a carjacking. I had no idea where that would lead me. I became an air traffic controller and somehow have spent of 30 years in aviation. I have so thoroughly enjoyed my career in aviation that the call of aircraft flying overhead always causes me to raise my head to the sky.

When I was speaking with a Hispanic community college administrator who was telling me that the majority of the Hispanic students she saw at her school could only see two career paths, either a nurse or an immigration attorney. She encouraged me to bring my fellow FAA employees to the school to talk to their students about their careers. She said, "No pueden ser lo que no pueden ver," which made me smile since I realized it also rhymed in English. "They can't be what they can't see."

Last year, we had a Minority Serving Institution (MSI) intern named Gigi, who was researching information on the NHCFAE. Gigi was from Florida and her family was of Dominican descent. I thought it would be fun to introduce her to a couple of our NHCFAE Latina leaders who were also of Dominican descent. One is a Technical Advisor in the New York District, the other is Aeronautical Engineer in the Commercial Space program. Both of them discussed how they came to the FAA and what they did. Towards the end of this meeting Gigi said, "It is so wonderful to see two women that look like me, doing the important work that you two do. It really inspires me."

Less than 4% of airplane pilots are female and Latinas are even rarer. Out of 17,783[1] FAA air traffic controllers, less than 17% are female and less than 1.7% of FAA air traffic controllers are Latinas. According to the U.S. Bureau of Labor Statistics, the median pay for a commercial pilot in 2021 was $134,620[2] . The

[1] https://www.transportation.gov/assistant-secretary-administration/human-resources/dot-onboard-demographics-june-fy-2022
[2] https://www.bls.gov/ooh/transportation-and-material-moving/airline-and-commercial-pilots.htm

median pay for air traffic controllers is over $129,000[3] . These careers can not only change the lives of the Latinas who attain these careers, but their families as well.

I have seen the dynamic power of careers in aviation and the effect it can have on generations of Latinos. Two of my predecessors as the President of the NHCFAE started while they were still in school. Faviola Garcia joined the FAA through the Stay-In-School program at the age of 16 and she is currently the AWP Acting Deputy Regional Administrator. Sadie Perez joined the FAA through a college internship program and is currently overseeing the Workforce Development Program for the Air Traffic Organization's Technical Operations. But maybe even more importantly, the example they set has led two of Faviola's children and Sadie's sister and two nephews to also attain careers in aviation. A career in aviation can not only be life changing, it can be family changing.

"No pueden ser lo que no pueden ver," to me, that is the greatness of the book, *Latinas in Aviation*. In this book young Latinas can "see," so maybe one day they can "be." This book features the stories of Latinas in the "DMV" (the District of Columbia, Maryland and Virginia). It has the inspiring stories of so many Latinas and their journeys to amazing careers in the wonderful world of aviation. It chronicles their stories, their struggles and their ultimate successes in the growing and fascinating industry of aviation. Not only will the readers learn about how Latina pilots and air traffic controllers got their start

---

[3] https://www.bls.gov/oes/current/oes532021.htm

and succeeded in their careers, but you will also read about the several other aviation careers that help ensure our national and worldwide aviation system is safe and secure.

Last year, at the First Annual Latinas in Aviation Global Festival at the College Park Aviation Museum and Airport in Maryland, I met a young Latina named Belen who worked in real estate in El Monte, California (not far from where I grew up). She had been so inspired by reading *Latinas in Aviation* that she had started taking flying lessons at her local airport. Belen had taken a red-eye flight from California just to attend the Latinas in Aviation Global Festival. When she met Jacqueline Pulido, the first Latina pilot for Volaris Airlines, and Jacqueline Ruiz, the author/pilot, Belen was overcome with emotion. That is the power of "pueden ser lo que pueden ver."

Administrator Huerta motivated me to reach out to young people about careers in aviation, especially young Hispanics. *Latinas in Aviation* focuses on young Latinas who gain power to lift and inspire generations of their families through the beauty of flight.

William (Bill) Fernandez
*FAA Aeronautical Information Specialist
Former National Hispanic Coalition of
Federal Aviation Employees (NHCFAE)
President and Chairperson of the NHCFAE
Charitable Foundation*

11

INTRODUCTION

I believe I have the best job in the world. Museums are incredible spaces for learning. Museums provide countless opportunities to learn about all aspects of life. Whether it is history, nature, science, art, music or sports, museums offer glimpses of our shared humanity. My job has allowed me to meet individuals from all walks of life and to share stories of people making an impact in their communities and the world.

My background is as a public/community historian. I have been blessed to work with minority communities, immigrant communities and communities of color. Most of my professional work has been uncovering unknown community histories, collaborating and sharing those histories with the general public. I never imagined that I would be leading an aviation organization. I was never a science person; I enjoyed learning about people, places and events—history. However, these short two years at College Park Aviation Museum (CPAM) have had a critical impact on my career. I have had the privilege to connect with many passionate individuals across the aviation industry. Pilots, instructors, engineers, air traffic control, mechanics and much more that want to share their story with others. I have also learned about so many individuals who have made College Park Airport a world-renowned location.

The history of our aviation campus is awe inspiring. However, I have also become more knowledgeable about the gaps and needs in aviation. There is a lack of diversity within the industry especially among women. Women and Latinas make up a very small percentage of the industry and yet they are one of the largest demographics in four-year universities. It can be discouraging not seeing someone like yourself in the career you want to explore. It has also been a challenge to people, like me, and cultural institutions, like museums, to understand how our work, interpretation and exhibits can hinder or empower our community in engaging in our work.

When I first arrived at College Park Aviation Museum, I looked at our exhibits and interpretation and did not see any connection to our Latina/o community. It made me think about the role of Latina/os in the aviation industry. I thought about the challenging work ahead. How would CPAM be able to connect with or inspire our Latina/o community if they do know see role models that look and speak like them in our gallery? It was at that moment after many conversations with Jackie and the coauthors that the vision of Latinas in Aviation Global Festival came to be. Here was the opportunity to connect our community to passionate women wanting to share their stories of perseverance, grit, arduous work, commitment and success. When the day came, it was an incredible moment that added to the history of College Park Airport. It could have been easy to say mission accomplished, but community building is never officially done. The question arose of what more could we do to create a more meaningful relationship with our community.

Every Latina donated an object relating back to their aviation career to the museum. Making history was not enough, we wanted to document and preserve history. I am happy to say that we have a Latinas in Aviation permanent collection for future museum exhibits. Latinas in Aviation is now embedded in our airport history for everyone to be inspired. But that was not all. Seeing the inspiration of last year's event motivated something even bigger, this book. Seeing the engagement of the local high school students, young children, the Naval cadets and our community residents was an awe-inspiring moment. Because of this, College Park Aviation Museum has the honor to be part of something bigger, Latinas in Aviation (Maryland Edition). This edition will connect you to Latinas who are breaking barriers, transforming the industry, inspiring many and are LOCAL, in your back yard.

I have always credited mentors for having a major impact on my professional career. Mentors offer ears to listen, words of advice and, often, challenging demands for us to achieve the best of ourselves. This book is for you Maryland (D.C. and Virginia). Our Latina/o community is growing in the DMV. I hope you find these stories inspiring and along the way find a mentor that is willing to help you achieve your dreams!

Lastly, I am excited about the Latinas featured in this book. It is easy to think of just pilots when you think of aviation jobs. However, this book includes the many jobs of aviation. You will read stories of engineers, architects, CEO's, students, flight instructors, operations managers, air traffic control, examiners, collections specialists and much more. The book will share the vast opportunities awaiting in the industry. I want to say a big thank you to all the women in the book for your willingness to share your stories and support the next generation of aviation professionals. Your impact will be felt!

Kevin Cabrera, Museum Director

College Park Aviation Museum

AUTHOR
CHAPTERS

WHATEVER THE WEATHER

FRANCES M. VELAZQUEZ

CURRENT POSITION

Air Traffic Control Specialist—Aviation Weather Subject Matter Expert

FAVORITE AIRCRAFT

Lockheed Martin Vega 5B

FAVORITE QUOTE

"Never underestimate the power of a girl with a book."
– Ruth Bader Ginsburg

FUN FACT

My three favorite childhood books were about flight: The Little Prince, The Story of a Seagull and the Cat Who Taught Her to Fly, and Jonathan Livingston Seagull.

Maybe it's an occupational hazard, but I think I have a lot in common with the weather. I think of myself as changeable and adaptable to different environments, and it began when I was young. Growing up in Ponce, Puerto Rico, my parents were very encouraging and open about letting me try new things. If I wanted to join a new extracurricular activity, I had to try my best, practice hard and finish out the obligation (the season or the show) before I could try something else.

I tried many different activities and quickly found out my preferences. I loved volleyball, basketball and track. I remember loving dance, but not ballet class. Instead, I found joy in a folkloric dancing group. The theater was an even better fit. I always did my best, worked hard, and I eventually realized that it was fun to mix things up. While in high school, I formed a dance and theater company with my friends. Going about this way helped me find out what I really wanted to do.

It makes perfect sense then, that my journey to my career was a winding path. I tried many things to get where I am. My current title is air traffic control specialist and aviation weather subject matter expert, but I am neither an air traffic controller nor an operational meteorologist. Instead, I am part of the Federal Aviation Administration (FAA) Flight Service Safety and Operations Policy Team. There I help guide emerging policies, safety standards and the strategic direction for the Flight Service Program. It's a career I enjoy, although it was not initially on my radar.

CULTURE SHOCK

In high school, everyone expected me to go into communications after graduation. I loved performing and could also give a great speech. But when I was 11, I had the opportunity to visit the Kennedy Space Center on a family vacation. That visit sparked an interest in science and technology that stuck with me.

After high school graduation in 2000, a good friend of mine was accepted into the Air Force Academy to study aerospace engineering, and I too began considering that as a possible career. I had encouragement from my family since I had a few uncles and a cousin who were engineers. So as I looked into potential schools, I decided to apply to one of the best—Embry-Riddle Aeronautical University. A few months later, I was kissing my family goodbye and on a plane to the school in Daytona Beach, Florida.

I wasn't fully prepared for the culture shock. Although I had taken advanced conversational English classes after graduation to prepare for the move, there was still a surprising language barrier. I didn't speak unless spoken to and, where once I was a straight-A student and social butterfly, I began to struggle because I could not always understand the professors or my peers.

I also looked around and found that I was one of the only girls in the classroom. Although this is common in engineering schools, it was not something I had expected and I had not prepared myself for it. However, the biggest challenge was that I found my classes boring, and eventually I decided I didn't want to become an engineer after all. Instead, I changed lanes and joined the Atmospheric Sciences and Meteorology program.

At the time, Embry-Riddle's meteorology program was a minor field of study and very small. For me, it was the perfect major. Coming from an island in the Caribbean, I was familiar with extreme weather and wanted to learn more about its effect on aviation. I had found my place at the school, but I still needed to get over that language barrier…!

One day I went with a friend to an Olive Garden restaurant so he could apply for a job. They were so short-staffed that they hired him on the spot and asked if I wanted a job too. By taking that job, I was put into a position where I had to use my English regularly. My language skills and confidence took a leap and before I knew it the language barrier at school and work began to shrink. When I left Olive Garden, a few years after graduation, I had risen to the position of manager.

In 2004, I was in the second graduating class of the meteorology program and one of eight students; the year before there were only four. I was excited to start my career in aviation, but I didn't figure out what direction I would take for a few years.

A BUDDING CAREER

I remember my first single-engine airplane ride. I was overwhelmed by all the chatter on the radio during our flight. Some of it was communication with the pilot and some was not; I couldn't tell the difference. I never thought I would, or could, become one of those people on the headset, but that's eventually what I did.

A few years after graduating, a friend tipped me off to a

weather-related job as a flight service specialist at Lockheed Martin. I was excited to find an application for my education. My job was to interpret and translate weather information and identify threats for aviators. I conveyed critical information to general aviation pilots directly and gave them details about the risks of the weather and what to expect during their flight. I also corroborated information from different sources, filed flight plans, relayed clearances, and coordinated with search and rescue teams.

While working at Lockheed Martin, I moved up the managerial ladder to become an operational supervisor and completed an MBA. But since I was never satisfied, I looked for other opportunities and, in 2015, I landed at Jeppesen where I worked as a general aviation customer consultant. There I had some of my favorite aviation moments. I witnessed "the world's busiest airport for a week" during EAA AirVenture in Oshkosh, Wisconsin, and rode in a T-6 Texan aircraft with the team lead of the AeroShell Aerobatic Team at SUN 'n FUN in Lakeland, Florida.

In 2017, I returned to my weather roots when I took a job as a senior scientist at AvMet Applications, Inc. There, I did a lot of product analysis and served as a liaison between the National Weather Service and the FAA, which is something I still do today. I was exposed to several workgroups of the Radio Technical Commission for Aeronautics (RTCA) and the International Civil Aviation Organization (ICAO), which is a specialized agency of the United Nations that influences aviation around the world. I served as an advisor to the U.S. member of the ICAO Meteorology and the Information Management panels. I helped develop policies and standards that support the sustainable growth of the global civil aviation system and ensure equity in access to aviation safety and policy in third-world and first-world countries. I also added to my global network.

People began regarding me as a subject matter expert, especially in the area of weather. However, just as the world of meteorology extends beyond the person at the weather desk, the world of aviation extends beyond the pilot in the cockpit or the air traffic controller in the tower. Like a hurricane in the middle of the ocean, I decided to once again change tracks and, in my next position at LS Technologies, I worked as a program analyst on air traffic management and drone technology. It was a very technical position where I was helping advance drone integration, conducting special studies, research, analysis and planning demonstrations to showcase new capabilities. In 2019, I was proud to draft the summary report to Congress for the Unmanned Aircraft Systems (UAS) Traffic Management (UTM) Pilot Program Phase 1. I participated in this pilot program as a team lead and drafted the document, which reported the results of a series of demonstrations performed by the FAA UAS test sites to show the capabilities of UTM.

All this experience led me to accept a role at the FAA in 2019, where I continue to work with weather and drones, as well as policy, standards and safety. My current position came to me in the way so many others have—through my network. One thing I have learned from trying new things and working at several places is that it grows your network exponentially. I have a very large network of diverse people from many organizations and backgrounds. Even in my current position with the FAA, I often have people above my level reach out and ask if I know certain people in the aviation world. I'm proud to be able to make important introductions that eventually lead to great things.

RISKS AND REWARDS

I'm indeed a risk taker. Making a move to something new and untested has inherent risks. However, I think the greater risk is constraining yourself to only one thing when there is something better for you on the horizon. To young people I say that if there's something that interests you... go for it. Don't stress out about what you want to be, where you will end up or what other people think. I laugh and say that I've been working in aviation for nearly twenty years and still don't know what I want to be when I grow up!

I can honestly say that my status as a Latina or a woman has not held me back. I'm a lucky girl. Yes, sometimes I am in the minority—the only one in the room who looks or talks like me— but I never let this affect my passion for following my path, even if at times that path seems erratic to outsiders. I continuously look for professional and personal opportunities and never hesitate to change tracks when it seems like the right thing to do.

Had I not changed majors in college, I may never have found my passion for weather. Had I not moved to the FAA, I would not have found a new way to affect the world of aviation. In recent years, I've learned that the majority of general aviation accidents occur because of the weather. This is partly because pilots in flight school often do not learn enough about weather and how it affects safety and performance. To tackle this, I have decided to become part of the solution and am pursuing my private pilot's license with the goal of becoming a flight instructor. If I can provide more in-depth weather training to prevent the occurrence of even one accident, my efforts will have been worth it.

BLUE SKIES AHEAD

There is so much to learn and explore in life. Keep throwing the darts till something sticks. Spread your wings. Think outside the box. Change your forecast. I have no regrets about any position I've held or how much time I spent there before moving on. In every position, I have built upon my already valuable experiences which have prepared me for even more.

It's just like the activities I participated in when I was a child. None of them were a waste of time or effort, even if I wasn't good at them. I always learned about leadership, teamwork and how one person affects the work of others. Missing a team practice or a rehearsal affects the game or the production. The interdependence is the same in the professional world.

Today, I remain open to transformation and growth, just like the weather patterns in formation as we speak. I love that there is so much to do within weather and aviation, and I encourage anyone interested to explore the many career opportunities available. I am proud to help pilots understand the weather in their flight plan to get them to their destination safely. I am also proud to be a successful Puerto Rican woman in such a rewarding STEM career.

Frances "Frankie" Velazquez Mercado currently calls Leesburg, Virginia her home, along with her wine sommelier husband, Travis, their adorable English bulldog, Brutus, and their fearless cat, Gary. She is currently with the FAA and is regarded as an aviation weather subject matter expert in her role with the agency's Flight Service Safety and Operations Policy Team. She can be reached at fmvm83@ gmail.com.

NEVER GIVING UP THE DREAM

ERYKA SILVA

CURRENT POSITION

Republic Airways Pilot in Training

FAVORITE AIRCRAFT

Cessna 172

FAVORITE QUOTE

"As iron sharpens iron, so one person sharpens another."

—Proverbs 27:17

FUN FACT

I love nature, but I'm afraid of mosquitos!

It was 2017 and I was on a tour bus in India on my way to see the Taj Mahal. I was travelling alone for a couple months, attempting to find peace and reflection after my recent divorce. I shared the bus with a group of jolly men and women who were enjoying the trip even more than me. As we drove through the dusty streets I let my thoughts distract me. Despite the end of my marriage, I had built a good life and career in automotive marketing as a tour manager for auto shows, in positions with Ford and Honda. I didn't know what was next, but, as always, I was optimistic.

"Hey, they say everyone who comes to the Taj Mahal is searching for something," one of the women in the group turned to me and said. "What are you searching for?" I told her I didn't know, but when I asked about the group she was with she told me they all worked for the airlines. Everyone was either a pilot or a flight attendant.

I smiled as a familiar memory overtook me. "I used to want to be a pilot," I told them.

THE BIG LEAP

I grew up in São Paulo, not far from Congonhas Airport. My friends and I would gather after school and play "airplane." The boys would be pilots and the girls would be flight attendants or passengers. One day, I asked to be the pilot and the boys told me I was ruining the game. Frustrated, I went home and asked my mom why girls can't be pilots. "I don't think there are any," she replied. She didn't realize that with that answer she was making me more and more determined to become a pilot.

One day I showed up at the game wearing a pilot's hat that my uncle had given me. "This is your pilot speaking, please take your seats," I said. Everyone laughed, but I stood my ground and was captain for the day.

In 2010, I moved to the U.S. and took a job as a nanny. I didn't know much English, but by May I was able to get around fine. My parents thought it was a big mistake, but I needed to learn English and save for the future, so I felt it was the best way to achieve my goal. The family who employed me moved around quite a bit and I lived in both Michigan and Colorado with them. A few years later, I took a contract marketing job to supplement my income. Part-time led to full time and I kept rising in automotive marketing as a tour manager and then a field manager.

As the years went on and I grew and matured, my memories of childhood games faded away and I pursued other interests; nobody had ever encouraged me to become a pilot. I had almost completely forgotten my dream until that group on the tour bus in India talked about their lives in aviation and set me on fire. I thought about the consequences. I would have to leave my marketing career behind, come up with the money for flight training and, of course, go through the training itself. My new aviation friends told me I shouldn't consider these obstacles at all. They told me that by training in the U.S. I could find financial assistance and plenty of schools to help, including scholarships available for minorities. They told me that with my determination and passion, becoming an airline pilot was truly a viable reality and I would be foolish not to pursue it! They reignited what lay dormant within in me... my childhood dream to become an airline pilot.

As I was leaving India, I thought a lot about pursuing aviation and became more and more determined. I decided the only way I was going to become a pilot would be to jump in with both feet. I used the 17-hour plane ride home to Maryland to research flight schools and flight training. I got in touch with Women in Aviation and other groups to look for resources that would help me.

A few months later, in March of 2018, my sister Sabrina visited from Brazil. To this day she's one of my dearest friends and the person who always reminds me to take care of myself and try to lead a stress-free life. I also owe my first experience with aviation to her because she gave me a Groupon for my first discovery flight at the nearby Bravo Flight Training in Frederick. It was a rough flight, a gusty day where the pilot was pushing his limits, but I still loved it. I was so excited that Sabrina offered to go shopping so I could stay for my first ground training class— that same day!

Now there was no stopping me. During the next year, I worked with Chevrolet doing car shows and racing events, and saving as much as I could for flight training. I finished my private pilot's license at Bravo one year later, on March 24, 2019. Now I was ready to finish the rest of the ratings required for becoming a commercial pilot.

I thought about flying constantly, although there were times I had doubts and worried about my path. What if I couldn't make it financially and needed to stop training halfway through or, worse yet, failed training and got stuck with a hefty bill for a career I couldn't fulfill? But when my boyfriend, Peter, co-signed a loan so I could get approved for the funding I needed to continue training, I kicked those negative thoughts out of my head. I had waited a long time to pursue my dream and now I intended to finish!

INTO THE COCKPIT

In June 2019, I moved to Florida to attend Phoenix East Aviation Flight School and finish my ratings through commercial single. However, when we shut down for COVID in April, I moved back to Maryland and Peter. I returned to Bravo and used my Amelia Earhart Memorial Flight Training Scholarship and scholarships from Women in Aviation International and International Society of Women Airline Pilots to keep working towards my multi-commercial and instrument instructor ratings. Brenda, the owner of Bravo, was again my instructor, and once I got my instructor rating she hired me as an instructor. Brenda remains a great mentor who always encourages me to keep going and believed in my ability to make it to the airlines.

Working at Bravo, I was able to live in Maryland, meet other pilots in the area and continue my flight education. During that time, I also became involved with the Civil Air Patrol. I enjoy working with the young cadets there who are all interested in pursuing a career in aviation. It has been rewarding to share what I know and encourage them to follow their dreams. I strive to be that pivotal person in a cadet's life who encourages them towards a career in aviation.

As a Latina, I'm also proud to be part of a small, but growing group of aviators, especially from my native country. I love bringing positive attention to my heritage, and surprising and inspiring others with what I do. It also means I am part of an incredibly supportive group of women who come to my aid when I need it most. I specifically have two Latina friends and fellow pilots, one from Brazil and one from Argentina, who have been with me through some of my darkest days in aviation... like my accident.

It happened in 2020, shortly after I became a volunteer pilot for Angel Flight, which provides air ambulance services. On September 20, I was the co-pilot flying back from a successful patient drop-off when our 1967 Piper Cherokee Arrow experienced a mechanical failure and forced us to make an emergency landing. The investigation is still in progress, but let me say that both me and the pilot are extremely lucky to be alive. When I was in the hospital the night of the accident, one of the ladies I knew from WAI sent me a message to see how I was because she had monitored our frequency. Others reached out too, and that support system, when I needed it, quelled my feelings of loneliness while I went through such a traumatic event.

I suffered severe whiplash and headaches for months, which necessarily grounded me from flight. My September 25 checkride was rescheduled for October 20. Those weeks were filled with dark days and negative thoughts, yet I wasn't ready to hang up my wings. Instead, I felt like I had to get back in the cockpit as soon as possible or the fear inside which was trying to conquer me would win the day. All I wanted again was to be found fit to fly so I could get behind the controls.

Finally, the day came. Sitting in the cockpit again was scary, but I was determined. My two best Latina friends graciously offered to fly with me for support. I was fine during the rollout, but when the plane went airborne, I began to panic. My friends literally talked me down to the ground and I was devastated by what had happened to me. Would I ever fully recover?

Brenda diagnosed my problem as the aircraft. "Try the Cessna instead of the Piper," she suggested. She was right. I felt much better with the Cessna, which I still prefer to a Piper. The silver lining of the accident was that it made me a better pilot and a better, tougher, instructor. Nobody is allowed to solo on my watch unless they know the plane systems forwards and backwards.

HELP FROM MANY

I look back on my life and think about how—other than the accident—making the career switch from marketing to aviation was one of the scariest things I've survived. Even as I was working in marketing, meeting people at trade shows or performing demonstrations, I always thought how my experiences could translate to an aviation setting and, in hindsight, it did. People that know me outside of work may call me a "hot tamale," easily angered and emotionally explosive, but on the job I am a cool cucumber. My job in marketing gave me a very thick skin. It taught me how to accept criticism and not to let my emotions get the best of me.

My emotional intelligence also grew with my marketing work. I worked with many kinds of people and I learned to be collaborative, and get the best result, even if working with someone I don't particularly like or get along with. This was a great lesson I can now take into the cockpit with me. No matter who I'm flying with, I can navigate a peaceful working relationship.

These days I'm learning to fly jets! I recently left Bravo Flight Training and am part of Republic Airway's training program. I tell Brenda that the intensity of the training is like drinking from a fire hose! As always, when I have my moments of doubt about myself, she encourages me. "You haven't come this far to give up!" she says. And you know what? She's right.

It's through the help of each other that we can find the strength to reach our dreams. We will all have adversity, but we can all persevere if we continue to support and encourage one another. If you can make it through one thing, you can make it through something else.

In my case, being a pilot is deeply seated within me. It's

a passion and determination that has given me the strength to bounce back from a divorce, make a daring career leap, survive catastrophe and return to the cockpit, and come ever so close to my final destination—being an airline captain. If the group in the Taj Mahal bus could see me now, what do you think they would say? My guess is they probably would say the same thing my seven-year-old self in the airline captain's hat would say: "I knew you could do it!"

And I finally say, without hesitation, "Me too!"

Eryka Cristina Xavier da Silva is a commercial single and multi-engines rated pilot, certified instrument flight instructor and First Officer who will soon be a Captain for Republic Airways. She can be reached at erykacxs@gmail.com.

BLAZING A TRAIL IN THE SKY

LEENA CARVALHO

CURRENT POSITION
Naval Academy Graduate/Naval Air Station Pensacola Student
Pilot

FAVORITE AIRCRAFT
Lockheed Martin F-35

FAVORITE QUOTE
*"...we have to surpass ourselves every day, make every day undying.
Climb our own personal Everest and do it in such a way that every
step is a little bit of eternity. That's what the future is for: to build the
present, with real plans, made by living people."*
- Muriel Barbery, The Elegance of the Hedgehog

FUN FACT
I hope to someday hike the Pacific Crest Trail that runs from
Mexico to Canada.

Sometimes you don't know things are possible until you see someone else doing them. Other times, you have to be the trailblazer.

When I was young, I remember flying to Hilo, Hawaii, from our hometown of Fullerton, California, to visit my dad's family. From the first time I went, I loved the thrill of flying. I didn't exactly know how to make it part of my life, but my uncle did. He was in the Navy and a bridge to the military for me. He lived across the street with his two daughters who pursued the military too. One of my cousins is now commissioned after attending college and Office Candidate School (OCS). My younger cousin is in Marine ROTC and wants to fly. As I progressed through high school, I began to think that I too could become a naval officer.

My loving family was supportive of the goal, although my mom was very worried. I was always someone who sought out mental and physical challenges and I knew I had what it took. First, however, I had to get through senior year and the college application process.

THE JOURNEY BACK

Everyone had big plans after graduating from my all-girls Catholic high school. Ironically, I think my days in a single-gender environment prepared me well for my current environment, where I am often the only female in the room. Within the walls of my high school there was an aura of woman empowerment, and there my confidence and my assertiveness blossomed. It would be with me the rest of my life. In school, I was also a gifted soccer player and hoped that my athletic talent might help me secure a scholarship or at least a place at a good college.

I also noticed that in the past, a few girls from our school had been admitted to the Naval Academy. It was encouraging. So at the end of junior year, I applied to many schools I was well qualified to attend. I also thought about another "reach" school—the Naval Academy—but decided to hold off for now.

Around the same time, I played in a soccer college showcase in Las Vegas. It was an event frequented by college coaches and I had invited some from my top colleges to attend. I was in the middle of a play, passing the ball down the field, when a tall girl ran right through my knee, blowing out my patellar tendon.

As I exited the field in excruciating pain, I knew the injury was serious. I knew it would be a while before I would play soccer again. I just didn't know how it would affect my future or my dreams.

I was so grateful to my orthopedic surgeon and my physical therapist. Both of them knew exactly what to do for me to heal as quickly as possible. After my operation, I did physical therapy three times a week. Very slowly, I regained my range of motion and strength. Months later, I was cleared to run. Then, I began thinking about applying to the Naval Academy again.

Doing so meant completing their candidate fitness assessment (CFA). For that, not only did you need to perform a mile run, but pushups, basketball throws and various other feats of strength. I didn't even know if I could physically complete the test, let alone get the score they wanted.

The weeks dragged on and I still thought about the Academy. When the deadline to submit my CFA approached, I still wasn't ready or confident that I'd pass. I requested an extension and got it. I kept training, gaining strength every day. I worked hard and got coaching from one of the athletic trainers from my high school throughout the summer. Finally, one sunny day, when we both felt I was ready, she administered the assessment. I was very nervous about the mile run, but I did it. I didn't get my pre-injury time, but I hoped it was good enough. Perhaps the toughest part of the application process was over, I thought.

I also had to get a nomination from a congressional or senatorial representative. I was interviewed by a panel of past officers who had attended different military academies. During one of the interviews, I had pneumonia, but did my best answering questions about my future and why I thought I would be a good candidate. I have to admit that my experience with my knee was a witness to my resilience, determination and strength. In the end, I was fortunate enough to be sponsored by Congressman Ed Royce of the 39th District for my application to the Naval Academy.

At this point, I was a very late applicant and I wondered if I should even bother. Yet, with visions of jets in my head, I still had to try. I finally turned the application in during the spring of my senior year, but when April rolled around I had already sent in a deposit for UCLA and was all set to go there. Then, I received THE letter. I was accepted to the U.S. Naval Academy! I couldn't believe my eyes. Here it was. A ticket to fly. Maybe. But no matter what happened next, I felt like if I had gotten this far, I was ready for whatever came my way.

ACADEMY DAYS

I graduated in 2018 and headed to Annapolis. Naturally, I was one of a few women within a sea of white male classrooms and teachers. However, I can honestly say that being a Latina didn't really help or hinder me at the Academy. I was treated like everyone else, except socially. There was definitely a camaraderie among the boys. It did not include me and the few other women in our class.

Perhaps the most exciting thing about being at the Academy were the many different kinds of people I met. I met enlisted men and officers, people from my home state and those from across the country. Eventually, we all became a family. When we're deployed, I have family across the world!

When COVID hit, classes went online. The academy took pride in how smoothly they transitioned to online learning. Still, it was sad to be sent home during spring break of 2020, see graduation canceled for that year and miss flight training. Everything resumed in the fall and we played catch-up. The hardest part was following all of the rules set forth by the Academy post-COVID. I didn't fully appreciate why we had to be in dress uniform outside the classroom. The juniors and seniors had the privilege of wearing other clothes, unlike freshmen. I guess in retrospect they wanted to hold our behavior accountable to our service branch and be exemplary about following orders during COVID. I had entered the academy hoping to fly, but I was determined to keep my options open, even when I had a chance to see the power and excitement of the military planes. Many people think you need to major in aerospace engineering at the academy, but the truth is there are a variety of studies available. I am a quantitative economics major and I was still eligible to become a pilot.

However, the academy made sure I knew what I was getting into. Every summer we were given the opportunity to visit the VAQ-135, which is an expeditionary EA-18G Growler electronic attack squadron that deploys worldwide to support U.S. Naval expeditionary wings, allied/coalition task forces, Marine aircraft groups and U.S. Navy strike groups. The squadron is stationed at the Whidbey Island Naval Air Station in Island County, Washington. The Growler aircraft represents the most advanced technology in airborne Electronic Attack and is responsible for jamming enemy signals as the Navy's first line of defense in hostile environments.

I'll never forget the first time I climbed into the EA-18 jet, which is an F-18 jet outfitted with the electronic attack components. I sat in the EWO (Electronic Warfare Officer) seat, right behind the pilot. He took me up and showed me what the aircraft could do, tossing me around in barrel rolls, loops and low-level flying that just made me want more. It was the coolest thing I've ever done in my life and convinced me more than ever that I wanted to fly.

Back on the ground, I asked the maintenance officer of the squadron where the female pilots were. "We don't have any," he replied. "The last time we had a female here she wasn't from the Navy; she was from the Australian Air Force." I took time by myself to walk around the grounds and appreciate the surrounding natural beauty, including the fresh smell of pine and the water views. I asked myself if I could imagine myself stationed here as a Navy aviator. Yes, I thought.

ON TO THE FUTURE

At graduation, my parents were so proud that I had made it through and stuck to my dream. I had shown myself that it was possible to attend the Academy and blazed a trail for other young Latinas like me who are thinking about applying. My time at the Academy passed quickly and as of this writing, I'm still in pursuit of my dream. I am awaiting the start of flight school and I'm raring to go! I'll be moving to Pensacola, Florida, soon, but COVID has put everything behind there. Currently, there's a shortage of instructors so I will have to wait to start ground school. In the meantime, I'm open to the possibilities of the next two years and am so happy to join the ranks of the women who have gone to flight school.

It seems to me that more women are going on to flight training these days and I like to think that perhaps I am part of a new generation of women who are seeing aviation as an attainable goal. I recently heard about the Navy's first black female fighter pilot, LT Madeline Swegle. She first received her "Wings of Gold" in 2020 and is flying with a training squadron in Kingsville, Texas. It's amazing to think it took until 2020 for a woman of color to make it as a Naval aviator, but the example of women like her make everything seem more possible for me.

Seeing female role models succeed is so important. My mom is a lawyer and, although we don't share aviation in common, she too is often the only female in the room. She showed me the path to being persistent in your dreams and not letting anything or anyone get in your way. Today she's a partner in her law firm and I find that so inspiring!

It was influences like these, who came before me and showed me the possibilities, that kept me on track during my hardest times at the Academy. Although I pursued and completed the work on my own, I couldn't have done it without my inspirations and mentors. From my uncle and cousins to the female aviators I met at school, to my classmates and supportive family, I'm grateful to them all for believing I could complete my quest to become a Navy pilot. To them I say, thanks. I'm almost there!

Leena Carvalho is a 2022 graduate of the U.S. Naval Academy and is headed to Naval Air Station Pensacola to begin flight training this fall. She can be reached at lmc301@gmail.com.

Appreciate you taking the time to meet us and read our stories. Keep inspired and reach for the skies!

STANDING MY GROUND

KEANNE VALLEJO-HUERTAS

CURRENT POSITION

Air Traffic Control Specialist and Policy Analyst

FAVORITE AIRCRAFT

Antonov

FAVORITE QUOTE

"Set goals. Stay quiet about them. Smash The ^%$* out of them. Clap for your &^%$ self. Repeat." –Pilot Wings Mason

FUN FACT

My twin and I both work in the aviation industry.

In some ways, I have had a turbulent journey in aviation. Like many women born and raised in the Puerto Rican culture, all too often we must show others what we can do before anyone will believe we can actually do it. However, having to show, rather than tell, has always pushed me on to pursuing my dreams.

Perhaps being a woman contributed to some of the bumps along the way, but I've succeeded on the wings of my own passion and determination. In my journey, I'm grateful to have had unforgettable mentors and support from friends and family who all made it possible. Ultimately, I managed to achieve some of my greatest dreams in aviation, all through hard work and showing my value to others.

THE "GIRL"

My mother gave birth to twins but I was the "girl" and it made all the difference. My parents were very protective, so I was constantly with my twin brother, John, and not allowed to go anywhere alone. My brother was always there. I remember trying to bribe him with money and even offered to do his chores, just so he would leave me alone to go to a party or see a friend. I was hard-working, got straight A's and did most of the housework, yet he seemed to have all the freedom.

Many people I meet in aviation had an early influence on their interest. The closest thing I had to knowing someone in aviation was a middle school math teacher. He would sometimes explain math concepts with aviation examples and equations. The way he talked about aviation fascinated me, including his passion for it. My dream began to form. I wanted to fly!

I kept quiet. Everyone else expected me to become a teacher because I enjoyed tutoring kids around my neighborhood who were struggling with their studies and my mom was a public-school English teacher. My dad was a Chief Warrant Officer in the military, but had also studied to be a teacher. I wanted something different.

At the age of 17, I told my parents I wanted to attend Embry-Riddle Aeronautical University and become a pilot. They wanted the best for me and to help me reach my career goals, which meant my dad wanted me to become an orthodontist instead of a pilot. He felt he could help me set up with an orthodontist office, but he could not buy me an airplane. Neither of them wanted me to go away for school.

I obeyed their wishes by staying close to home and enrolling at Interamerican University in Bayamón, Puerto Rico. However, without telling my dad, I enrolled in the program of Airway Sciences and Management, which had a minor to become a pilot or an air traffic controller. It was a secret between my mom and me. It wasn't until I was well into taking my first year of classes when my dad noticed my textbooks were about aviation, not orthodontics. He was stunned. Not only because I had not told him, but because I was succeeding. It was then he realized how passionate I was about my goal. From that day on, I had his full support.

I loved my aviation classes and planned to take the pilot

minor, until I began learning more about air traffic controlling. The career seemed like a good fit for me, so I redirected my studies. I look back on that moment now as the best decision I've ever made!

I graduated from college in 2010. Like so many ATC grads, my next step was to await a call from the FAA to be offered placement into their training program. The wait list at that time was known to be several years long. So, I went on with life. I pursued a master's degree in psychology, figuring if being an air traffic controller didn't work out, I could help aviators with their mental health. I also planned a wedding with a man I had been dating for five years. The big day was December 23, 2012. Then two weeks before the wedding, the phone rang. It was the FAA.

"Keanne, are you ready to go to the academy?" the voice on the end of the line asked. My heart was in my throat. Of course I was, but what about the wedding? Quickly I asked them when I would have to report. Luckily, I didn't have to start until March. The wedding was still on, but I was only a few classes and a practicum away from earning my master's in the next semester. I had to make a choice between going to the academy or finishing my psychology degree. For me it was a no-brainer. I was going to be an air traffic controller!

NEW WORLDS

Being in Oklahoma with my new husband for FAA training was the first time I was in the States and also away from home without my brother or my parents. Having an air traffic control minor meant my training was cut in half, so I only had to be at the academy for three months. However, they were some of the most grueling, challenging months of work I ever encountered. At the end, I put in a bid to work at my desired en route facility and got my first choice placement: San Juan CERAP (a Combined En-Route Radar Approach Control Facility). I was going home.

From the first day I set foot in the CERAP, I could tell everyone was surprised the FAA had sent a woman. The men would offer me history lessons about my predecessors.

"Every time we get a woman they leave."

"We haven't had a girl make it here in 15 years."

Little did they know that instead of putting me down, they were challenging me!

Then John Figueroa entered my life. He was the "tough" supervisor and evaluator who nobody wanted because he was strict, asked a lot of questions and failed you for the little (but equally important) things. As luck would have it, I was assigned to him.

Classroom training was the first step in becoming a Certified Professional Controller (CPC), followed by on-the-job training (OJT) and then the certification exams. We needed to pass multiple "checkrides" –tests—to get certified. As a supervisor, John had high expectations and you could either strive to meet those high expectations or fail. He challenged and tested everyone equally and made no allowances for anyone. Gradually, I began to look at him less like a supervisor and more as a mentor. I believed he wanted us all to succeed and be excellent at whatever we did. I picked his brain and made sure that I went the extra mile since I knew many people expected me to fail. Training was tough, but I had amazing mentors that shared their knowledge and pushed me. I studied, stood my ground and persevered.

Unfortunately, as my career flourished, my marriage began to falter soon after starting my position in San Juan. The husband who had willingly supported my career goals thus far couldn't adjust to my erratic schedule, constant studying and unavailability, alongside his own medical school studies. For the sake of both of our well-beings, we decided to end the marriage.

The day I needed to appear in court was the same day I had a final evaluation for the classroom portion of my radar training. They offered to reschedule, but I pushed ahead. Fast forward to March 10, 2016, five days before my twenty-fourth birthday. I was certified as a CPC! It was so exciting. No other female had certified in the center since 2001, and it was the proudest moment of my life.

After achieving CPC, my team saw me as a greater asset. I became an OJT instructor and made it my mission to empower, teach, inspire and encourage new trainees to trust in themselves and the process. The aviation community can be ruthless and not unlike a sorority or a fraternity where you have to be inducted in order to "earn your stripes." Once you're in, it's a tight knit family, but women in aviation must always look after ourselves. We operate in man's world and must be our own advocates.

QUICK CHANGE

Shortly after my certification, I was at an out-of-town aviation event with colleagues. One night, a man I trusted forced his way into my hotel room. I found myself defending against a sexual assault before I got him out the door. Shaken and terrified, I tried to call colleagues for support, but nobody answered. I didn't feel safe. I had to get out. I called a friend in the area, spent the night there and flew home the next day. Like so many women in this position, I had to determine whether to keep quiet or press charges. After much thought and with support from family members, I took the difficult path and filed a report. I couldn't ignore what had happened.

There was an investigation and, in the end, the man admitted I was telling the truth. I was disappointed when he was reprimanded, rather than suspended, for his conduct. It meant I was expected to continue working beside him every day.

The stress of the experience took its toll. I coped by doing classroom training, rather than the OJT work I loved. I learned who my true friends were and I dealt with the negative backlash that came my way. Finally, I weighed my options to find a new path that would point me in a healthy direction. I have always tried to not live a life I was given, but instead live the life that I dream and work for. Nothing in aviation comes easy and we take great pride in our job because only the strongest and most determined ones make it through. I decided to start fresh by pursuing a goal I had considered long ago... working at FAA headquarters!

In 2019, a job opened up for an air traffic control specialist and policy analyst at FAA headquarters in Washington, D.C. Upon starting with HQ, I worked in support of the ATO (Air Traffic Organization) safety management system, primarily writing and executing safety risk management policy. Now, I work in operational readiness, collaborating directly with facilities to identify how they can respond to service outages and resume operations in a safe and efficient manner. I have some firsthand experience with this as I was one of a handful of ATCs dispatched off the island of Puerto Rico during Hurricane Maria to direct air traffic control operations. From Miami, our task was to perform ATC without radar. It was one of the most rewarding and memorable experiences I ever had.

We always look for the positive that comes from our negative experiences. I have learned that the union now trains and designates emergency contacts for offsite events like conferences. I like to think my experience and my inability to contact anyone when I needed help the most, may have contributed to that development.

I'm also married to a wonderful man I met in college. He is an aviation geek too, so he understands the demands of my career and is extremely supportive of what I do.

I have returned to Interamerican University to speak to and mentor budding women in aviation. I tell them to be committed to their goals and stand their ground against anything that gets in the way. To achieve great things in life, you have to surround yourself with people who will assist and support you unconditionally. With perseverance, a career in aviation is within everyone's reach.

Keanne Vallejo-Huertas is an Air Traffic Control Specialist and Policy Analyst based at FAA Headquarters in Washington, D.C. In 2016, Keanne smashed the glass ceiling of CERAP San Juan to become the first en route female CPC there in 15 years. She can be reached at kvallejoh@gmail.com.

REACHING OUT TO REACH MY DREAMS

ELIANA ROTHWELL

CURRENT TITLE

Aviation Student at Delaware State University

FAVORITE AIRCRAFT

Beechcraft 18 – my first flight and first cockpit I ever got to sit in
and fly in!

FAVORITE QUOTE

"If you never try, you'll never know." –**Germany Kent**

FUN FACT

I hated Indian food until I graduated from high school, bought a
one-way ticket to India and backpacked there six months! Now, I
love Indian cuisine!

I grew up with a very special photo album on the shelf above my bed. It's a photo of my adoptive parents and my sister, Danika, when she was four years old. They are standing behind a Mexican woman who is seated and about nine months pregnant—with me. It's a photo of my biological mother.

When that woman in the photo entered my thoughts, I would sneak down to the basement to the special box where we kept old records. I would take out my Spanish birth certificate and scan it for the name I had come to recognize—Susana Silva, my birth mother. I always knew I'd reach out to her someday.

That document was once my only connection to her. Little did I know that aviation was another one.

AN INSPIRATION OF AVIATION

My adoptive parents brought me from Tijuana, Mexico, to Durango, Colorado, where I was born and raised me with all the love and attention I could want. My dad was a goat farmer, while my mother was a doctor by day, farmer by night. For about ten years, we would grow and sell what we could at the farmer's market. At first it was flower bouquets, but then goat's milk and, eventually, artisan cheeses. These days, my mom does floral design for weddings and has even done some for celebrities, like Lily Collins.

Growing up in a smaller town, I didn't have much exposure to aviation. However, when wildfires broke out in the neighboring forests, I was fascinated by the firefighting planes that swooped in and saved the day. I always wondered what it would be like to sit in the cockpit, but I didn't know any female pilots or women in aviation except for one—my mom's friend Joan, who was a pilot with United Airlines. I only saw her on rare occasions, but heard about her travels.

Joan became more of a mentor as my journey in aviation progressed, but my main aviation inspiration came from our neighbor, Joe. He was a private pilot and owned his own Beechcraft 18. He moved into our neighborhood after my high school graduation. I met him at a time I was open to various career paths and enrolled at the nearby Fort Lewis College. Joe could see my interest in aviation; so one summer day in 2018, he offered to take me up in his airplane. I found myself intensely fascinated by everything in the aircraft—the controls, what every button did and the special language he used that all pilots knew. As we soared over my hometown, I was hooked. Once back on the ground, I immediately applied to Delaware State University (DSU) in Dover to enter their program of aviation.

Why DSU you may ask? I had relatives in the area and had enjoyed so many childhood visits there. DSU also fit my qualifications as a HBCU (Historical Black College or University). Durango had little diversity in its population, so I was looking for the opposite in my college experience. I didn't want to be the only person who looked like me in the classroom.

A month later, I received my acceptance from DSU. I sat my parents down and told them I wanted to enroll in the aviation program. They were supportive, as always, but figured my interest in aviation was just a phase, like so many of my other occupational interests had been. It wasn't. So in 2019, my mom and I packed up the family car and took the drive across the country to pursue my dream.

The next summer, Joe, who I now considered my "Godfather of Aviation," flew me in his plane to the Experimental Aircraft Association (EAA) show in Oshkosh. There he introduced me to some inspiring women in aviation, including a 747 pilot he knew. My inspiration and determination to have a career in aviation continued to grow.

Back at school, I pursued my private pilot's license and then had an opportunity to attend the 2020 Women in Aviation International (WAI) conference, sponsored by DSU. The experience was a true turning point in my life. Seeing and meeting women from all over the country who had succeeded in such a male-dominated field gave me a feeling of empowerment. I can do this, too, I thought. I returned to school energized and ready to continue my flight training. And then… COVID hit.

TAKING OFF WHILE GROUNDED

Just when my excitement level was at its peak, all flight training was grounded and academics went online. While I matriculated quite nicely with my required academic courses, I was disheartened by the lag in my flight training. I couldn't wait for the world to open up again. The WAI conference was virtual that year, but I was already thinking about attending the 2022 conference and also how to bring WAI to my area. We had no chapter, so I decided to start one!

DSU was very supportive, but we all agreed we should wait until the lockdown was over to hold meetings. Classes finally resumed in August 2021. It was a privilege to be back in the cockpit, but I also went full steam ahead with creating a new WAI chapter.

I had never started anything big before. I reached out to the WAI for instructions and they sent me everything I needed. I quickly learned how to run a nonprofit at the age of 23! I had to get an EIN, establish a permanent address for when I moved out of state, get articles of incorporation, fill out tax exempt forms, pull together a board to create bylaws and open a business bank account. It was a lot of work but I was determined to get the new Delaware Diamond Chapter off the ground.

Pulling together interested participants was a slow process, but eventually a board of committed aviation students joined me. We discussed our mission and decided that our chapter membership would extend beyond DSU to professionals throughout the state. We reached out to ladies at the nearby Dover Airforce base about joining and many were interested. We also decided our chapter would include a diverse cross-section of the aviation industry, to include air traffic controllers, airport managers, etc.

Next, I reached out to the aviation program to sponsor us to attend the 2022 WAI convention in Nashville, Tennessee. I was so looking forward to seeing the ladies in my chapter get inspired like I did at my first conference. Then, DSU told me they could not sponsor us because COVID restrictions prohibited them from sponsoring any out-of-state student activity.

I was crushed.

When I told the board, it was already February, a month before the conference. I thought we would just have to skip it this year... unless... I had a sudden realization.

"We're not allowed to fundraise as a collegiate chapter, but we are not a collegiate chapter," I told the board. "Do you think we could fundraise the money in enough time?"

The girls were willing and we all went into high gear. Our only restriction was not to use the college's name in our fundraising efforts. First, we reached out to alumni, family and friends through a Go Fund Me account. We raised $5,000 in the first week! We continued by reaching out to different airlines for support. Alaska, Piedmont and United Airlines all gave us indirect donations by covering the cost of student registrations or airfare. We also received an amazing donation of $5,000 from Amazon. It was very important to me that we raised enough money to cover not only the entrance fee, but the plane fare, hotel and out-of-pocket expenses, as we were already financing our flight training with loans. Our goal was to send eight interested girls to the event and amazingly, in three weeks we raised $13,000, which was enough to cover all necessary costs. It was the WAI Delaware Diamond Chapter's first triumph and would always make us proud!

Our chapter grew from nine aviation students to 25 community professionals. We meet monthly and have an aviation book club, and are fundraising for scholarships and registrations for the 2023 WAI Conference. We also can't wait to share our love of aviation with the next generation and participate in our first WAI Girls in Aviation Day in September 2022.

Getting the chapter launched and on its way was one of two great accomplishments from reaching out to others during my college days. Now, I'll tell you about the second one.

MEETING ANOTHER MOM

During my first semester at DSU, I thought a lot about Susana Silva. I was a little scared to reach out, but felt like it was the right time in my life to finally meet her. My mom was nervous and wanted me to be prepared for all possible outcomes. I assured her I was.

I was able to locate her on Facebook and I sent her a message with the news that I was her daughter. She welcomed me with loving, open arms and told me she had been waiting for the moment when I would reach out to her.

In the summer of 2019, I traveled to Tijuana to meet not only Susana, but her entire extended family, including my aunts and younger cousins. Seeing her in person after weeks of communication was surreal. Susana had given me up when she was 21, but had never told her family. I was a complete surprise. Susana had no children of her own at all; after my birth she had tried, but had been unsuccessful.

I communicated with her through a translation app since

she did not speak English and I only knew a little grade school Spanish. She told me that giving me up had been heartbreaking, but she had been unprepared and unsupported, and decided her baby would have opportunities elsewhere that she could not possibly provide. She was currently the director of finances at the Paul Mitchell hair care brand, but told me she loved to travel and had wanted to work in the airlines. She had even applied to be a flight attendant many years ago, but had not been accepted. This unexpected aviation connection between Susana and me warmed my heart and was somehow comforting. Perhaps my love of aviation sprang from Susana and the opportunity to embrace it was made possible by my parents, just as Susana had hoped.

Today I continue my journey in aviation and my work with our WAI chapter. Currently my academic work is done and I only need to complete my CFI, CFI-II and multi-rating to finish my program.

I am also aspiring to the Aviate program at United Airlines and am partway through the process. The program works with aspiring aviators to provide a pathway to work as a pilot for United Airlines. For me, it would be a dream come true to work for United. I admire their commitment to increasing their workplace diversity and their passion for creating a more sustainable aviation industry. It was also one of the few airlines that serviced Durango when I was growing up.

I'm flexible and open to where my journey will take me, and also inspired and open to the mentorship of the women who have paved the way in aviation. I tell young women interested in aviation not to give up, even if they don't immediately see a mentor. It wasn't until I was in college and went to EAA and then WAI when the world of aviation possibilities opened up for me. Reaching out to role models and mentors and staying involved is key. There are many of them waiting for you to reach out, which is always a good thing in our professional life, as well as our personal one.

Eliana (Ellie) Rothwell is currently a student in the Department of Aviation at Delaware State University and the founder and current president of the Women in Aviation International Diamond Delaware Chapter @waidiamondchapter. Ellie can be reached at rothwelleliana@gmail.com.

ADVENTURE TURNS INTO PASSION

RAQUEL VILLAGOMEZ

CURRENT POSITION

Diversity and inclusion project coordinator

FAVORITE AIRCRAFT

A380 and Airbus BelugaXL

FAVORITE QUOTE

"Stay the course."

FUN FACT

I lived in Cochabamba, Bolivia, from 8-14 years old and didn't know Spanish before moving there. I became fluent in Spanish by being put into an all-Spanish-speaking school called "Colegio Tiquipaya."

Before I was born, my mom wanted a better life for her family. She arrived in the United States, crammed in the trunk of a car with five other people and lucky to be alive. She was seven months pregnant with my sister.

She sacrificed for us, working hard for every dollar she earned. Some might have been beaten down by it, but my mom is strong and has inspired my three sisters and me. She taught us courage, resilience and kindness, and always told us, *"cuando uno quiere, puede.* If you want, you can."

My adventure began in Fairfax, Virginia, where I was born and lived until the end of third grade. It got more interesting when we moved to Cochabamba, Bolivia, and I had to learn Spanish. We lived there until I was 15 and then moved back to the United States before my freshman year of high school.

When I was growing up, I was adventurous. As you might expect, my mom understood my personality well and always had a vision for me. She knew I wouldn't follow in my sisters' footsteps in the medical field or law. It became clear to her that I wanted to do something more unique and out there—an adventure! So, she talked to me about being an astronaut, saying, "Imagine how cool that would be, going into space."

As we talked about the future, my grandpa also thought I should be an astronaut, but my dad disagreed. He was adamant that I should be a pilot, saying it fit my personality. My dad had always wanted to be an airline pilot, but he could never achieve those dreams. This became a special father/daughter moment and we began dreaming about my goals together.

Living in Bolivia meant there weren't many role models for me. I didn't see many women in powerful positions, especially something like being an airline pilot. The industry is very male-dominated, not only in Bolivia, but everywhere. My parents wouldn't put up with the notion that aviation wasn't for women. My dad would take me to the airport, making me sit in the car, close my eyes and imagine how powerful an airline pilot must feel to be in control of such a big aircraft. That vision stayed with me throughout all my years in school. It was engraved in my mind; I was going to be in aviation—an airline pilot.

When I came back to the United States to begin high school, it wasn't long before I was asked what I envisioned for my career. What are you going to do? What school are you going to apply to? My mom always said, "You can do whatever you want. If you want to be an artist, you can be an artist, but you must get your degree, so if anything were to happen, you could use it."

So, I applied to Embry-Riddle Aeronautical University. I was accepted, did my flight training and got my bachelor's degree in aeronautics with a minor in business administration. When I went to school, I insisted that I wanted to do flight training and become an airline pilot, so I completed training and received my private pilot's license. I'm able to fly a Cessna 172, which is a single-engine aircraft.

DIVERSITY AND AVIATION

Throughout my flight training, I noticed some diversity issues that I was curious about. During my flight training journey, I knew I needed to do something else, something even bigger than being an airline pilot. I had noticed there was a huge lack of Latina pilots. (This was the year before the first Latinas in Aviation book was released.) When I started doing a lot of research, I discovered we had no resources. There was nothing in general for women in aviation and, even more, there was nothing specifically for Latinas like me. That's when I dived into researching diversity and inclusion (D&I) within the aviation/aerospace field. It wasn't long before I knew I needed to be a part of making a difference for minorities.

In my junior year of college, I reached out to the Latino Pilots Association, a group that supports Latinas in general and pitched an idea. I said, "There needs to be a support system for us. What can I do?" They were very supportive and gave me the go-ahead to create a subcommittee called ELLAS (Empowering Latina Leader Aviators), a support system for Latina pilots.

Upon graduation in December 2021, it was time to look for a job. During my previous research, the issue of D&I kept rising to the top and is something I became deeply concerned about. As a result, I dove back into my research, this time looking at commercial airlines. I noticed a new movement in the aerospace industry. Airlines were looking to do more with D&I and I decided to take a risk, deviating from my original goal to pursue a job that I was passionate about and would be fulfilling because I would be making an impact.

PASSION, MEET JOB

This led to the job I started in March of 2022 as the diversity and inclusion project coordinator at Airbus. What that means is internally and externally, I work to further D&I efforts. As an example, we have seven employee resource groups (ERG), such as Pride, Full Spectrum, Women, etc. I coordinate events for these groups, ensure everyone is aligned, and help them reach their goals.

Externally, part of my job is coordinating conferences that we attend from the ground up. For instance, Full Spectrum is an ERG on racial diversity. They're part of the backbone for conferences like the Society of Hispanic Professional Engineers (SHPE). I'm in the background, making sure that we have the right Airbus employees attending these events and coordinating conferences overall.

I also work with customers like United Airlines or Jet Blue. I collaborate with them for things such as Hispanic Heritage Month. I coordinate with each airline and have separate events for Hispanic Heritage Month. One that we're planning is a panel discussion with airline pilots and mechanics to give them a chance to talk about their experiences.

What I like most about my job is that I can learn so much. I know that D&I is a big passion for many people, but I believe that it goes beyond passion. It takes constant research to say on top of all the D&I topics.

It's exciting to have a fantastic boss who gives me the freedom to make this role my own. She's very supportive, but lets me figure it out, which makes me grow as an individual and an employee. We were talking one day about how amazing it would be to add a diversity and inclusion course to an aerospace or aviation degree—required for graduation—because, all too often, the individuals pursuing those degrees aren't exposed to D&I history, issues and statistics. She gave me the go-ahead and suggested I work with someone else who is passionate about it, too.

It's a lot of hard work, but worth it. That's why I changed career paths to make an impact and help minorities in aviation and aerospace.

GET OUT OF YOUR COMFORT ZONE

When you look back at your career path it isn't going to be linear. Always remember that it's okay to deviate from your initial goals. I'm the perfect example of that. Changing my career path and pursuing something that wasn't as clear as being an airline pilot took me outside my comfort zone and changed my life. It also grew my confidence because achieving my goals was powerful, even if it seemed sporadic. If I didn't go down the path that I did, which was initially going through the airline pilot pathway, I wouldn't have gotten to the place that I wanted to be, which is D&I within aviation and aerospace.

Being a Latina in the aviation/aerospace industry is a different experience for each of us because we all have different backgrounds and personalities. I've distilled this into a series of words rather than describing it as a story. I believe words hold power and those I think of when it comes to my place as a Latina in this field are perseverance, strength, uniqueness, groundbreaking, powerful, persistence, determination and resilience. Those are the words I used, relied upon and made a part of my journey. I think they relate to everyone that is in aviation, especially Latinas.

HELP OTHERS, BE A MENTOR

As an undergraduate student pursuing flight training, I observed many improvements that needed to be made for minorities in general. For example, not having any type of resources, such as groups, to help minorities to succeed in aviation, where we can empower each other or talk about our difficult situations and find guidance.

Before the first volume of this book, I didn't hear about any type of vulnerable topics being discussed about Latinas and aviation. Reading the first book and seeing how their stories connected with other Latinas was comforting.

I hope that one day my career will be focused on mentorship specifically. Obviously, my career has just begun, and you never know where you'll end up, but that is my ultimate goal—to be that mentor, to be that hand for others going through flight training.

While I strive to reach my goals of helping others in meaningful ways, there are three things I am proud of today. First, my inaugural solo flight. I still remember all the feelings I had, all the adrenaline and being in complete control of the aircraft.

In my mind, I returned to my dad talking to me and reminding me how powerful this would feel. I felt that strength and that power within me after all the stress, the checklists to ensure safety, talking with air traffic control and being able to take in the moment, flying with no stress. I'll always cherish that moment.

The second is when I obtained my flight training certificate. That's when you become a private pilot and you can take people flying. It was rewarding and reassuring that I was on the right path.

The third moment was during graduation when, as senior class president, I was given the opportunity to speak at graduation. To talk about my journey and have the chance to acknowledge the hardships my mom went through and how hard she worked just so my sisters and I would have food to eat was very emotional. It was especially rewarding to thank her for everything she's done for me to be there that day, giving my speech.

As you follow your path, remember it's not linear. It may have twists and turns, and if you end up in a different place than you planned, some say you have failed. But I don't think that's the case at all. I believe things can change. You may find other things that spark more of your interest and your path may deviate. Accepting that and being okay with new opportunities is always positive and something I'll always push for.

If you decide that aviation is for you and flight training is a part of your journey, it will be challenging. Sometimes you'll feel like you don't belong there or that this isn't the right career for you. The people there might not look like you and you might not be able to relate to them. I hope you realize that no matter what boundaries, stereotypes or statistics are against you, you can overcome them all.

Raquel Villagomez is a diversity and inclusion project coordinator at Airbus. She can be reached at rachel.villagomez@airbus. com.

AVIATION ARCHITECT AVIATRIX

LUCIA MENCIA, AIA, PMP

CURRENT POSITION

Aviation Architect

FAVORITE AIRCRAFT

My own little Cessna 172

FAVORITE QUOTE

"There's more to life than being a passenger." -Amelia Earhart

FUN FACT

I told my CFI that the "wind gods" commanded that I solo on April Fool's Day and did so with a fourth, power off, glide landing!

I had been assigned to an architectural project in Fort Lauderdale, Florida, for six months and the Airbnb I was staying in was across the street from Fort Lauderdale Executive Airport (FXE). I would see little planes taking off and landing all the time, and I decided to walk across the street to investigate. In what seemed like only moments, I was tucked into a Cessna with a certified flying instructor (CFI) from Colombia on a "discovery flight." He pointed and said, "Do you see that puffy cotton ball cloud over there? And that one? Well, I want you to go over the first one and under the second." I hopped over and dipped under and that was all it took! It was absolutely magical and I was hooked!

I spent the next six months juggling work with studying Jeppesen, federal aviation regulations (FAR), taking Federal Aviation Administration (FAA) trial exams and taking flight lessons. It was a great mix of learning and experience—a wonderful combination of what I thought were magic elves that kept the plane in the air and scientific motors analysis. Airborne Aviation Academy at FXE had many foreign students taking advantage of the cheap gas and severe clear Florida weather, so I made many lifelong friends with Colombians, Venezuelans, Brazilians, Australians, Germans and some from the UK.

I was all alone in Florida, so I would do my work in the mornings and then walk across the street. I was making great friends; a group of us would buy a giant pizza and study in the evenings. When pursuing a degree in aviation, you have to study thick binder books and doing it together made it easier and more fun.

As I look back over the years, it's clear that flying has broadened my vision of life and of this world more than any other thing. It has allowed me to mentor young people, Latinas and experience events that non-pilots would not understand. Some of those experiences include flying over pine-covered mountains near Spokane, Washington, and seeing slivers of silver lakes from a perspective that only a pilot sees, flying over the Everglades and seeing nesting alligators, and flying over the Lower Marlboro Wildlife Reserve to help count endangered ospreys—something I never knew was done. Every chance I have to fly is fantastic, but these experiences have been very special.

Other opportunities took flying to a new level of awe and excitement. One of those was the chance to fly in the old Powder Puff race—now the Air Race Classic—over Texas, Montana and Nebraska. It was during this race that the spectacular glory of this beautiful country was exhibited for me—buttes, mountains, valleys and long stretches of desert.

Another time, on a trip to Spain, I got to fly over the Alhambra and was amazed at the hectares of olive trees and many castles. On a trip to Greece, I got to fly over many isolated and exquisite islands that still house only their mythical Gods. In France, I flew over some of the castles in the Loire Valley, which makes them look like grand doll houses.

Pilots are blessed to see God's beautiful earth. Never does a pilot take Mother Earth for granted. If you haven't considered learning to fly or have been on the fence, I hope sharing these experiences helps you visualize and dream of a new future. As a pilot, you will discover that you are in control of much more than you realize, and it will become a great source of self-respect and strength.

This is your chance to get out of your comfort zone and know that you can do something most people will never attempt.

FROM ARCHITECTURE TO AVIATION, A LIFETIME OF EXPERIENCES

In my profession, I've had a unique opportunity to mix work and passion. I design and work in aviation architecture and am president and owner of Aero-Biz Development Group, which provides a wide range of services, from airport construction and master planning to promoting aviation grants and giving technical advice on FAA airport improvement projects. Starting my own company came from working in airport architecture for another company and a project at Dulles International Airport (IAD) in Dulles, Virginia. For that project, I was assigned to Dulles Airport as task manager on re-location constructions that were required due to the construction of a new fourth runway, 1/19 at IAD.

For five years, we labored to relocate existing buildings, including the weather station, some of the buildings for Federal Express and a new fire station on the IAD campus to avoid conflict with the new fourth runway. Five YEARS before the target date, I announced at progress meetings, where IAD ATC was represented, "Hello, I am Lucia, a pilot, and I want to be the first GA landing on the new runway." For those five years, I ended each project report with that annoying tagline.

Then, on the morning of November 20, 2008, in my little C172, I took off from Manassas KHEF and at approach to Dulles and the new runway, I didn't hear the customary "cleared to land" with my tail number, but instead, "Lucy, you are cleared to land!" I loved it and had a giggle attack while setting up to land. I was the first general aviation pilot to land on the new fourth runway at Dulles on November 20, 2008. MY runway. My colleague engineers and airport planners held a party for me at the Signature FBO when I touched down and my logbook has the autographs of many of my colleague architects and airport engineers who worked on the project with me.

I've discovered that not only is being a pilot exhilarating, but it can also add humor to your life. We were working at the Morristown, New Jersey, airport and I had a scheduled program scope meeting, so I flew in from KVKX and landed. I then phoned the contact for the meeting and politely said, "Excuse me, I am at the FBO and I know that our meeting is somewhere on the airport campus, but I don't know which building. Would it be possible for you to pick me up at the FBO, please?"

A grumpy, unhappy voice answered, "Well, okay."

The general manager picked me up and we went to the meeting, where one of the airport managers looked me over, top to bottom. He then asked, "So, where is the aviation architect?"

When the GM explained I'd flown in, the manager said, "So?"

The GM tried again. "No, she flew herself in!" After that, the result was instant credibility, a few chuckles and a very productive relationship. In fact, the manager insisted on a detour to Lucy's Sweets, the best homemade ice cream shop, before I was returned to my airfield plane.

As an aviation architect, it is valuable to be able to say: "As a pilot, I know that you need to have this navigation aid here because of wind shear," or, "No, you can't put the lights here because the pilots won't be able to see it easily," or, "Let's talk about NAVAIDs," or, "We need to think of pilot-controlled lighting." Those are the things that I'm able to offer as a value due to my knowledge as a pilot and it makes a big difference.

Imagine being asked if you would like to be involved in construction management for the new Air Force One hangar. My immediate answer was YES! The project was at Joint Base Andrews Air Force Base (KADW) for a new hangar to house a new Air Force One, VC25B, the military version of a Boeing 747. This is an enormous hangar (366,000 SF) costing about $250 million with a length of 660', 575' feet in width, and a height of 115'.

The width of the building is due to the aircraft having a 225-foot wingspan. Official Department of Defense documents say, "The hangar evokes a sense of flight and stateliness through its use of materials, massing, and embellishments." This reflects the fact that this is an environment that's a far cry from the cluttered halls familiar to most aircraft maintainers. It has been humbling to work in an environment of national and historical importance.

I've also enjoyed working on the new terrazzo compass rose in front of the Vega airplane and 99s memorabilia of Amelia Earhart's exhibit at the Smithsonian Air and Space Museum.

TRANSFORMATION IN FLIGHT

Aviation has transformed my life more than anything else. It's broadened my life through new relationships and new opportunities. My Christmas card list is made up of a lot of aviation friends, including women pilots who are members of the Washington 99s, the association started by Amelia Earhart.

Being a contributor to the aviation community has opened doors and provided opportunities I would not have had otherwise. It has allowed me to give back to many different communities. I serve as president of the Washington 99s, Washington, D.C., Chapter, vice president of Women in Aviation, Blue Ridge Chapter, and am a board member for the College Park Aviation Museum and the Experimental Aircraft Association, College Park Chapter.

It has been a pleasure to contribute to them and many other aviation organizations. I also greatly enjoy my time spent mentoring young women aviators. I cannot imagine a life without being a pilot. It is life-changing and having the chance to encourage others to "find their wings" is one of the most rewarding experiences.

A rewarding opportunity came when, as program co-director of the Build a Plane program, I developed a program for 30 British International School high school students who successfully skinned and took apart a fabric 1952 Piper Pacer airplane. As part of the program, I taught general aviation, aviation mechanics and restoration mathematics. Under supervision, the students restored fabric, seats, aviation panels, avionics wiring and the windshield.

I helped to motivate and build teamwork amongst the students, who also successfully restored the tailwheel airplane to flying condition. Each of them achieved an increased understanding of applied mathematics, geometry and construction materials. Best of all, I was able to inspire two high school girls to study for the FAA pilot's exam and continue to earn their own FAA flight wings.

I cannot describe how rewarding and joyous that was, to impact their lives in the very best way. Every time I have an opportunity to mentor others, as I do yearly at the Women in Aviation conference, I see these young women who start out quite shy and reserved, unsure if they can do it. After we spend time together, I can encourage them, help them understand that they have the power and they can follow their dreams to be successful.

I am grateful to be part of a profession that encourages this. I have never felt excluded because of my Cuban heritage and Latina background.

DON'T LIMIT YOURSELF

When I mentor others, I always tell them that they should not limit themselves and don't let others limit them, either. You are capable of more than you think! And you will find flight to be mind-expanding and healthy!

You have an opportunity to expand your education, your experiences and to set new goals that might seem ambitious. Don't hold yourself back. You can do it! Yes, it takes a lot of work, but you will grow. Learn to dream big, trust yourself and do your best. Amelia Earhart also said, "What do dreams know of boundaries?"

Lucia Mencia is an aviation architect whose professional credentials include a Bachelor of Science degree in economics and finance, a Master's degree in architecture and post-graduate certifications. She can be reached at LMencia@Aero-BizDG.com.

NORMA-BAT SHEVA ORONA-SAMMS

CURRENT POSITION

Static and Dynamic Structural Analyst at Boeing

FAVORITE AIRCRAFT

F/A-18 E/F Super Hornet

FAVORITE QUOTE

"Be fearless in the pursuit of what sets your soul on fire."
–Jennifer Lee

FUN FACT

I powerlift. To date, I have deadlifted 225 pounds while weighing 102 pounds.

My journey to aviation was not conventional. Parenthetically, my name, my upbringing and life experiences have also never been conventional. However, it is within this unconventional story, that I became an Afro-Latina in Aviation.

I was raised by a strong-willed, proud Mexican mother and a creative, adventurous Jamaican father. To those who know them both, it is no surprise their children each have names with a unique history behind them. The first of ten children, my mother left Mexico and her job as a chemical engineer at age 25 to pursue a future in the U.S. Her path to citizenship was made possible by a Jewish woman who employed her, named Bathsheba. A month before I was born, her best friend from high school in Mexico passed away from cancer. Her name was Norma. My name, in turn, is a combination of two meaningful women in my mother's life. My full first name is NormaBat-Sheva.

I was born second out of four children. Daniel, me, Francesco, and SaharaImann. My older brother, Daniel, is the strongest person I have ever known. Since birth, Daniel has been severely handicapped, confined to a wheelchair and can't walk, talk or eat on his own. His plethora of medical problems have taken him in and out of hospitals periodically throughout my life. A great deal of responsibility for him was given to me as "the oldest." Although we did have at-home nurses who also provided care, Daniel's medical needs increased over time, and caring for him was always a responsibility shared between me and my parents. My family counted on me to be there for him.

Growing up in New York City to a heavily in love Mexican-Jamaican couple was certainly unconventional, but beautiful. Spanish was my first language until I learned English in kindergarten. My father enamored my mother with his smooth demeanor and curious creative mind. At the time, my father created jewelry and sold it in festivals all over New York City. As a hobby, he would build radio-controlled (RC) model airplanes and would spend time piecing parts together to make the perfect aircraft and fly them around our apartment. Looking back, he provided me with my first inspiration of engineering and aviation.

Today I work in aerospace engineering, but I did not travel the traditional path to get there. I made it with hard work, getting to know myself, serving my family first and a little bit of luck.

FOLLOWING AN INSPIRATION

When I was seven years old, 9/11 hit and our family was forced to move from New York to Orlando for financial reasons. My most impactful memory was visiting the Kennedy Space Center for the first time. Seeing the mighty space shuttle, Atlantis, suspended gloriously from the ceiling filled my imagination with visions of the astronauts aboard. I also had an even more thrilling vision—me aboard. Yes, my seven-year-old self decided I was going to become an astronaut!

The feeling to explore space was strong and is still with me today; although I am an engineer, not only by career, but by mindset. I believe humankind holds an innate drive to create and engineering provides the structure to do so. As an artist knows his/her own flow to give life to abstract ideas, so does the engineer who uses the language of math, science and imagination.

For me, that language did not come easily. Still, in elementary-middle school, I always put it upon myself to get stellar grades and was admitted to a rigorous college-level program in high school called Cambridge. Thanks to amazing teachers, I developed several skills and interests, such as communication skills through literature and a strong foundation in physics. However, pressure to perform well and my vision to become an astronaut was suffocating. As you can imagine, receiving a "C" on a math exam easily becomes devastating when you are ultra-focused on a STEM career. Negative talk sets in and you begin to wonder if you are really destined to pursue a career in aerospace engineering. In hindsight, I now know these failures never defined me. Overcoming failure helped me refine my learning process.

During my senior year, I received a Women of Excellence scholarship to Embry-Riddle Aeronautical University. However, my mother just started nursing school and I was needed more than ever at home to care for Daniel. Also, even with the generous scholarship, I could not afford tuition. With a heavy heart, I enrolled at Florida International University (FIU). FIU did not offer a bachelor's degree in aeronautical engineering, but I decided to stay at FIU and pursue mechanical engineering.

THE CONFERENCE CONNECTION

While attending FIU, my parents were often busy with school, work or with Daniel, so I would often have to take my little sister, Saharaimann, to class with me. She was seven years old at the time.

She grew up attending my college classes and activities, learning her multiplication tables and about non-Newtonian fluids in my thermodynamics class. We were warmly welcomed to the Aerospace Engineering Club. Led by passionate juniors and seniors, we learned about planes, rockets, and the process to design, build and fly RC planes made of balsa. Saharaimann would come and learn, building her own sculptures out of balsa alongside me until ten o'clock at night.

I joined the Society of Hispanic Professional Engineers (SHPE) at FIU in 2016. Upon hearing about their upcoming engineering conference in Seattle, they convinced me I was certain to find a summer internship there. Huge aviation companies were going to attend and would be recruiting new talent including the top three on my list: Boeing, Lockheed Martin and Northrop Grumman. I dreamed of interning at any of them, but as I critiqued my resume I worried it was not impressive enough.

My GPA was okay, but I knew I would be competing with 4.0s. Also, I had no true work experience. I had organized a gala for my church's mission trips and was in the aerospace engineering club, but I had never received a paycheck. All I had was extensive experience in health, childcare and practical hands-on experience programming RC airplanes from home. Early on, my parents and I had made a pact that my first job with would be directly related to my major. Now I felt great pressure to walk away from that conference with an internship, no matter what.

When I walked into the room of recruiters, it was loud and crowded, but I was determined. I moved from booth to booth introducing myself. Nothing definitive happened, except when the representative from Northrop Grumman politely told me I didn't have the GPA they were looking for and to try again next year. I felt myself becoming discouraged. How was I supposed to leave with an internship? Was it hopeless? I needed to take a break, away from the crowd.

I bought myself an ice cream, went outside and sat down. Soon after, a girl sat down next to me who I assumed was another student attending the conference. Her name was Stephanie Cavazos and we began talking. We had some things in common. She was a Latina who juggled many responsibilities along with her classes and we shared similar stories. Before long, I found myself pouring out my heart to her, telling her about my dream and how I felt I really belonged there, but how I was so different from the other candidates. Then, she revealed her secret.

"Sheva, I'm a second-year intern at Boeing and I'm supposed to look for good potential interns. Can I see your resume?"

I couldn't believe it! Stephanie said she would present my resume and tell the people I needed to speak with the next day to expect "a girl with big hair," (which was how she described me) to stop by. Stephanie was as good as her word. The next day I made a beeline for the Boeing booth and found the people who had seen my resume. I gave them my best spiel on why I would be a great intern. I was encouraged that they listened, but they didn't offer me an internship.

Still, back at home, I didn't give up. I stayed in touch throughout the holidays, with greetings and updates on what I was doing to show my interest. Then, in February of 2017, they requested an actual interview. I told them about my intense homelife and they were genuinely interested in how I juggled everything. In the past, I had kept that part of me hidden from others, but now I see how it distinguished me from everyone else. My GPA was understood and didn't tell the whole story of my passion and desire to work in aerospace. Now I tell young people that if everybody takes the same courses and has the same degree, what distinguishes you from other people? The answer is your whole experience and the skills and passion you bring to the table.

SHPE taught me that if one recruiter doesn't like you, go to the next one. Yes, it's important to work on your GPA and build your resume, but if something is not perfect, it doesn't necessarily mean the door is closed. YOUR story is important.

I am so happy Boeing took the time to consider what was left unsaid on my resume. I was offered a summer internship, including money for relocation. I would be working on F/A-18s (the fighter jets used by the Blue Angels) at the Naval Air Weapons Station China Lake in California. It was a miracle for me and it involved a number of firsts. The first paycheck job. The first time I had to relocate, away from my family, and the first time I had to travel alone. I drove two hours from the airport, through the Mojave Desert (much of the time without cell service) to get to the Naval base. I was on my way!

GROWING AT BOEING

I was ecstatic for my new adventure, but also felt guilty leaving the family. That first summer was a transition for all of us. In the program, I was one of six interns and one of two girls. We became very close and I learned so much from the other engineers and pilots. I was invited back for the next summer as a flight test engineer intern and tested new software being implemented in new aircrafts for the Blue Angels. I also had access to Navy pilots, who could recommend me to Officer Candidate School (OCS). I was still thinking about becoming an astronaut and since many of them started out as fighter pilots, I knew OCS would provide a path. But after having heart-to-heart talks with the pilots, I learned of the great sacrifice that it took to go that route. I also acknowledged how much I already loved what I was doing. Slowly, I felt a shift in my trajectory as I realized that working for Boeing as an aerospace engineer was where I wanted to be.

After my third internship year and then graduation, I was delighted to be offered a permanent position at the Boeing Philadelphia Design Center and am happily working there today. Now, I strive to be the mentor that I never had and inspire young people looking for careers in aerospace. I meet middle school students and I'm amazed to see them using software programs that I did not experience until college!

I am still just as fascinated as my seven-year-old self by our place in the universe, the miracle of our very existence and what space travel would be like. And, like my younger self, I still think I may get to space someday. Now, thanks to companies like SpaceX,

Blue Origin and Virgin Galactic, today's astronauts can be teachers, geologists and artists. It would be quite like me to get to space the way I got to Boeing—in an unconventional way. Stay tuned.

NormaBat "Sheva" is a structural analyst at Boeing. She can be reached at contact@shevaoronasamms.com.

FLYING LIKE GEORGE

MELISSA TORRES

CURRENT POSITION

Contract Jet Pilot, Designated Pilot Examiner, CEO of
Advanced Aviation Group

FAVORITE AIRCRAFT

Super Decathalon

FAVORITE QUOTE

"Don't dwell on your mistakes—learn from them and move on."

FUN FACT

I earned my scuba diving license with my eldest son and then got
to dive in and clean the Baltimore Aquarium.

I was never supposed to be a pilot. I was supposed to be a doctor, like my father and so many other people in my family.

My parents moved from Paraguay to Philadelphia, when my father changed medical specialties from internal medicine to urology. My two little brothers and I grew up in a loving family, the first-generation in the U.S. When it came time for college, I went down the pre-med route, like everyone expected. But about that time, I got my first glimpse of a cockpit and I never forgot it!

We were travelling from Argentina to Paraguay during a trip to see our grandparents, before 9/11. A kind pilot saw my intense interest in the front of the plane and asked if I'd like to see the controls. He even let me sit in the cabin during take-off! I thought it was the most amazing thing I'd ever experienced! Little did I know that one day I would not only fly small and commercial planes, but also helicopters and even serve as an examiner for the FAA. The aviation adventures would come my way, slowly, but surely.

GEORGE

After my first two years in college, I switched my focus from pre-med to economics and Spanish, which were majors I was able to finish in the four years. But college did not douse the desire to pursue aviation. I thought about joining the military for flight training, but I didn't have 20/20 vision. Instead, I half-heartedly took a job as a financial analyst.

Then one day, I was out with friends and met my husband,

Dave. Believe it or not, he was in medical school with plans to join the service upon graduation. We were married and eventually moved to Washington state so he could start his duties. There I met another doctor's wife who was also a general aviation pilot. When I asked her how she got her license and she told me about private flight schools, I couldn't believe it! I had no idea you could learn to fly outside of the military.

Soon we were relocated to Newport News, Virginia. It was hard to keep up the financial career with all our moves, so I took other jobs as I could get them. Then one day in 1996, I decided it was time to scratch my itch to learn to fly. I went to the nearest regional airport and walked in to inquire about taking flight lessons. That's when I met George.

He was the most amazing aviator I ever met. George flew P-51 mustangs in World War II and he was quite the storyteller. The first time we got in the cockpit, he motioned towards the instruments.

"You don't need any of this s&*t!" he said. "You just fly."

George was from that rare breed of aviators that flew by their gut and their instincts, not their instruments. George believed in intuitive flight and taught me rare skills that I still use today, like how to listen to the sound of the engine, be aware of what the plane is doing and the importance of the feel of aircraft. He believed that when you weren't flying in instrumental conditions, looking at the instruments too much could slow your reaction time and distract you. Flying instinctively was often the best choice.

George learned to fly on a single-seater aircraft. One day I asked him how he learned to land without an instructor next to him.

"On a blackboard," he replied.

"What!?" I answered incredulously, realizing this meant he had to land a plane the first time without an instructor. "Weren't you scared?"

"I didn't think about it until I was up in the air," he said. "I was 19 and stupid."

Can you imagine learning to land like that today?

I did things with George that other instructors "taught me" how to do in my more advanced flight training, like daily spins, landing an aircraft with the engine cut and doing real approaches, where you land the plane using only instruments, very early in my training. George is no longer with us, but he left an indelible mark on my heart and gave me an amazing start to aviation. I feel like he's always with me in spirit, whenever I'm in the air.

CLOSE CALLS

I said goodbye to George when we moved to Washington, D.C., and I was forced to find another flight instructor at the Marine Corps Base Quantico to start working on my commercial license. At the time, I was pregnant with my first son. I decided I would keep flying, as long as I could, but wait to do my long cross-country flight which was necessary for my commercial rating.

One day when I was in my second trimester, I went up in the T-34 airplane to practice flying slowly. For the maneuver, I needed to put the gear down and watched for the three lights on the console which indicate that the wheels were down, but the indicator lights didn't go on. I used an emergency crank, but still could feel nothing definitive. I listened and only heard the motor. I radioed the tower and asked them if they could check my wheels on a fly by. After passing them the tower told me they could see my wheels were down, but not locked. I tried everything I could think of to force the wheels into proper position, but I knew nothing was working.

As calmly as I could, I told the tower my wheels were most likely going to collapse as I landed. At this time in my training, shutting the engine down was the protocol so I knew there would be no fuel flowing in case there was a fire. I opened the canopy so I could make an easy escape. In other words, I was preparing for disaster for me and my unborn child.

If I make it through this, I will learn something, I thought resolutely. Then I looked down on the runway and saw policemen and a fire truck, ready for a crash. All eyes were on me.

I began my descent as if this were a typical landing. I did one of my best three-wheel landings and then, as predicted, I felt the wheels of the aircraft collapse. I held tight. The aircraft slid along its belly for about fifty feet to a gradual stop. And I was fine. Wow, I thought. I did it. In an instant, the firefighters were running up to me, dressed in their silver fireproof suits, yelling at me to get out of the cabin. In a moment of quick-thinking, I grabbed my log book.

They whisked me to the ambulance and took my blood pressure. I didn't tell them I was pregnant or they would have surely hospitalized me. The newscasters were on their way and I could also imagine the headlines, "Pregnant woman makes emergency landing." No way! As soon as I could I called Dave and told him if he hears anything about an emergency landing in a T-34, it was me and I'm fine. I felt just like George, because he could land in any situation. He would have been proud.

I kept flying into my seventh month. The birth of my oldest son stopped me for six weeks, but then I was itching to fly again. One day the flight school called to tell me my usual plane was down for 100 hours of maintenance, but the T-34 was back online and available for practice. I was tempted because I was so close to my commercial rating, but I wasn't sure whether I should try a long flight without my preferred aircraft. I decided to wait.

That day the instructor took someone else up in the T-34. There was an engine failure upon departure and when they tried to turn around and land the plane, they were both killed.

Suddenly it seemed like every time I was ready to get back in the saddle, there was a plane crash. John Denver. JFK Junior. I was surrounded by bad aircraft karma everywhere I turned.

NEW AERIAL PURSUITS

It was time for another move, this time to North Carolina, and I was pregnant again. I was too busy for flight school. Then another move back to Washington, D.C. I was home for 15 years, raising my family, until my youngest went to kindergarten and I went back to work. I took a job in finance and hated it. I wanted to return to flying, but how? I was 43 years old.

Near my house there was a helicopter school, so I decided to learn to fly those instead. It was fun, but expensive, and in the end I only flew for five hours. I told myself I needed to get myself back into a plane and catch up with my training if I was going to fly for an airline. I enrolled at ATP in Florida and planned to be gone for a month. It was tough on the family me gone, but ATP's program was intense. Between the eight hours of classroom daily and the intention to have a checkride on the fifth day, I actually completed my commercial license much earlier than expected. Then, I built hours in the multi-engine airplane. I returned home with my commercial rating. I then got my CFI, CFII and MEI at ATP in their two-week program. Afterwards, ATP called and encouraged me to work for them as a CFI, CFII and MEI. At the time, you did not need 1,500 hours to work for the airlines, so I got a job at a regional, but they were not paying enough to offset the disruption of the family.

Back in Frederick, the owner of the helicopter flying school, Neal, asked me to join them and we struck a deal that he would help me find and purchase an aerobatic plane. I still have my Super Decathlon. Neal asked me to teach for him, but not in such a beautiful plane. I got my helicopter license and I was hired to fly the JetRanger helicopter for a survey company, in addition to airplanes. For a few years, I was the survey company's main pilot. Neal became a fixed-wing FAA examiner and got very busy.

Knowing my background in finance, he asked me to help him run Advanced Helicopter Concepts.

Meanwhile, the Frederick Flight Center was a family business that was in decline. They too asked for my help in running the business. I could tell from the books there was mismanagement, so I offered to run it for a year to see if I could turn it around. If I could, I would pay all the debt and not take a salary, but I would receive part of the business. If not, the company would need to declare bankruptcy. We struck the deal.

In the end, the team of Neal, myself and Chris, another aviator we both knew, saved the flailing flight school and became partners running it. I handle finances, Neal lands the contracts and Chris handles operations. It's a terrific balance. We run the company as Advanced Aviation Group, dba as Frederick Flight School. I also run Fly for Fun, LLC which is my leasing business for my Decathlon and I'm also involved with Fly for Fun Aircraft, LLS, which leases helicopters back to the flight school.

If that doesn't keep me busy enough, I also am now an FAA examiner, which was an offer too good to pass up. Who knew that at the age of 54 I could marry finance and aviation in such a unique way?

I am so happy to have had the time to raise my three boys and then build a career in aviation and do what I love as a profession. I remember back to the day I met George and his incredible style of aviation. I tell my flight instructors that older students should be treated with respect because it's never too late to become a great pilot and pursue a career in aviation. I'm living proof!

Melissa is an entrepreneur mother of three, contract jet pilot, designated pilot examiner and CEO of a flight school in Frederick, Maryland. She can be reached at melissator3@yahoo.com.

FLYING INTO A CAREER AT THE SMITHSONIAN
NATIONAL AIR AND SPACE MUSEUM

ELIZABETH GARCIA CORVINGTON

FAVORITE AIRCRAFT

C-150

FAVORITE QUOTE

"You can often change your circumstances by changing your attitude."
—Eleanor Roosevelt

FUN FACT

I have a soft spot for dogs, especially senior pups.

When it comes to the top 10 museums in America, the Smithsonian National Air and Space Museum (NASM) in Washington, D.C., comes in at #5, according to Forbes. As chair of the Collections Department at NASM, this is something my staff and I are proud of.

In my role, I lead an exceptional and dedicated staff across four units: Preservation & Restoration, Conservation, Registrar's Office and Collections Processing. They are housed in multiple locations, including the National Mall Building in Washington, D.C., the Steven F. Udvar-Hazy Center in Virginia, and the Paul E. Garber Facility in Maryland. I oversee all aspects of collections management, conservation, documentation, shipping and storage within my department. My primary responsibilities are to protect, preserve and provide accountability for the national collection of aircraft, spacecraft, related artifacts and works of art.

We have more than 75,000 artifacts in the national collection and those on display inspire wonder and awe in our visitors each day. Their enthusiasm and excitement reflect the same feelings I had when I first visited, and still have to this day. NASM houses an expansive display of artifacts—everything from a space shuttle to small pins—and while it's tough to choose a favorite, I do love our art collection. We have some magnificent and beautiful pieces.

As I write this, we are at an exciting time in the history of NASM. We are getting ready to reopen the first eight of 22 galleries of our transformed museum on October 14. This has been a monumental effort that began in 2017 and, as you can imagine, my department has been at the center of it. There has been more to this effort than I can describe here, but the results are incredible. You can visit our website at www.airandspace. si.edu to learn more.

Accepting a job here was not my first experience at NASM, but it was a direct result of the first time I visited. I had been given an airline ticket as payment for my internship with Pan American World Airways and I used it to fly from Miami to Washington, D.C. The whole purpose of my trip was to visit the museum. I stayed with a friend and I remember it was freezing cold, there was snow everywhere. I spent the entire day at the museum and loved every minute, reading every exhibit label, speaking with the staff and meeting people. The next day I went back to Miami with a career goal of one day working there.

I started at NASM in 2004, having met Don Lopez, our former deputy director of the NASM years before when he was a guest speaker at my university's homecoming. I considered him a mentor and kept in touch with him throughout the years. When the opportunity presented itself, I applied for my current position and was thrilled to have been selected.

LOVE WHAT YOU DO AND IT'S NOT A JOB

Alan W. Watts once said, "This is the real secret of life—to be completely engaged with what you are doing in the here and now. And instead of calling it work, realize it is play."

Looking back at the road that brought me to where I am

today, I think of my mom. I was always interested in aviation and loved going to the airport. Back then you could walk up to the gate and get a close look of those magnificent jetliners. Often, she would take me to watch airplanes take off and land at the airport in Miami, where I grew up.

During my last two years of high school, I had the chance to attend community college where I completed my two-year degree along with my high school diploma. I had studied business, but wasn't certain in which direction I wanted to go. I decided to follow what always interested me and went back to college to take some aviation courses. I loved all my classes and knew I wanted to be a part of this world.

That was all it took. Love and fascination, together with education and reading about early aviation history, deregulation and commercial aviation, set me on the path to my future. I began by completing that two-year degree and then attending Embry-Riddle Aeronautical University, where I earned my undergrad and MBA as well. I chose to study something I loved, as opposed to something I was told I should. As a result, I love what I do—especially working with people who share the same interest, passion and are as devoted to the mission of the museum as I am.

When you stop and look at all the incredible history around us, of how far humanity has come, it revives your sense of wonder and fascination. Very few people get to interact with these incredible pieces of history the way the museum staff does, let alone on a daily basis while at work. We are fortunate to have this opportunity.

FULFILLMENT ON A MOLECULAR LEVEL

Working at NASM fulfills me at a molecular level. In the same way some people are into cars, my passion has always been aviation. It's an integral part of me. I've always enjoyed airplanes regardless of the size, style or time period—I've enjoyed everything about them.

When I was the director of the Museum of Aviation in Georgia, I had a chance to ride in a B-1 Bomber. We were at Warner Robins Air Force Base, where part of the Georgia National Guard is housed. They gave me the fastest ride I've ever had. We went from central Georgia to Savannah—about 165 miles—and out over the water, where they do their practice and maneuvers in 15 minutes flat. It was exhilarating and quite the ride. It was such an exciting experience—one I will never forget!

A SENSE OF WONDER EVERY DAY

My workplace includes spaces that house artifacts from space and early flight history, such as the 1909 Wright Military Flyer and others that showcase general aviation, including aerobatics, racing and gliders.

Working in this environment gives me a sense of wonder every day and it has undoubtedly changed my life, giving me a rewarding career in the process. It has allowed me to work in an environment that I love and has offered me some great opportunities as well as challenges.

The challenges sometimes included being a woman and a

Latina in an industry—aviation and aerospace—that traditionally doesn't have a lot of people who look like me. When going through school and at the beginning of my career, I was wholly focused on my goals—one after the other. I knew there were obstacles, but I focused on moving forward, believing I could do it, and achieving all I dreamed of. As I near the end of my career, I continue to see the full value of mentoring and the importance of telling stories of everyday women and everyday Latinas.

THE IMPORTANCE OF ROLE MODELS

There are some great female role models from the past, but I think we need to share those stories that are more commonplace and may influence and speak to a younger audience. My mom was an incredible role model for me. She was a single mom who worked hard and I saw that. I saw some excellent examples of how to stick to your guns and focus on doing better. She always wanted me to do better than she did. To move forward, study hard and have a career.

She left Cuba while in her early 30s during the revolution and I remember her passion for education, she often spoke to me of the importance of having a degree. She would say, "They can never take your education away from you. You'll always carry that forward with you."

I believe that she was right. My education provided some good opportunities and allowed me to compete and grow. I hope that as things shift, more women and Latinas will have better opportunities. It's been exciting to have the chance to do so many things throughout my career that I never even imagined, and to meet and work with some excellent people.

Being a Latina in the aviation and aerospace field means I have a great responsibility to other Latinas and women. Whether you realize it or not, you are always an example for others. I remember how I used to look up to women who I thought were successful in life and thinking she's doing that or saying this, or holding back or behaving this way. I never had a mentor who told me what to do or say in a boardroom, but I read a lot and educated myself. Today, I'm in a place where I am glad to give back, to stop and have a conversation, or share what I've learned with others, and I think that's important.

FOLLOW YOUR DREAMS

If you are interested in aviation as a career, you must be true to yourself. If aviation is what you love and want to pursue, then you should. Following your dreams isn't always easy, but it's worth it when you reach your goals.

There have been many challenges throughout my career, but I was able to persevere. I did that by reminding myself that working in this field made me happy and that deep down inside, I was satisfied and loved what I was doing.

No matter what challenges you may face along the way, remember you aren't alone. Don't be afraid to reach out to someone, a woman or Latina in aviation, if you need help or have questions. I've done that and have received great advice.

You have a great future ahead of you if you choose aviation, where you will be happy, satisfied and fulfilled. That desire in your heart? Follow it and, when an obstacle comes up, figure out how to get around, over or through it, because your goal lies ahead waiting for you to claim it.

Elizabeth Garcia Corvington is chair of the Collections Department, at the Smithsonian National Air and Space Museum in Washington, D.C. She can be reached at garciae@si.edu.

SOMETIMES IT IS ROCKET SCIENCE

KAREN PEREZ

FAVORITE AIRCRAFT

SpaceX Falcon Heavy Launch Vehicle (A rocket, of course)

FAVORITE QUOTE

"Your attitude, not your aptitude, will determine your altitude."
— Zig Ziglar

FUN FACT

I went plant-based during the pandemic and I love it!

When I was 17, I had surgery to realign my jaw. As part of the healing process, my mouth was wired shut for six weeks. It was a process that I found fascinating, that such an invasive surgery could have such amazing results in the end. That influenced me to want to be a dentist and I declared a biochemistry major in college with a pre-dental concentration. As easy as it was to take that path, though, several classes I took made me question whether it was the right choice. I'm a big picture person and these classes focused on the tiny pieces inside of other tiny pieces, inside of cells. I'm generalizing, of course, but when it came right down to it, it was too granular for me.

I needed something that could intersect passion with skill (and specifically after getting a particularly low grade in my biology midterm), I opted to take a career aptitude test, thinking it might offer some guidance. My results were culinary science, architecture, electrical engineering and aerospace engineering. I thought, "Hmm… I like airplanes," and without hesitation switched my major to aerospace engineering.

It's a bit funny because if that seemed like an abrupt decision, it was. I didn't do enough research, at least not how I would've done it today, especially when making such a big change. But, once I took those classes, I was enamored and knew I'd made the right choice.

Switching majors, I wasn't the absolute best student (though I certainly studied like I was), and I think that's important in and of itself. The education system can sometimes push us to the point of questioning if we're good enough to be there. At the end of the day, none of that matters. What matters is that you do your best and get your degree, which essentially gives you the tools you need to be successful in your career.

In my experience, the Latin culture can make personal growth a challenge. People in my family still ask, "Are you a pilot?" I explain that I'm an aerospace engineer and they don't always know what that is. Others will say, "Airplanes, huh? Well, let me know when you're flying an airplane, so I don't get on it."

This may be why throughout my journey, I've questioned myself. Am I capable? And after many years of asking myself this, I've concluded that yes, I am. I've had to shift my perception of what intelligence and success are. Growing up Dominican-American in the Bronx, New York, you had to *"ser vivo,"* or be astute and think faster than others—especially in a low income community riddled with crime and poverty, otherwise you were labeled as incompetent or seen as an easy target. I've had to unlearn this as I've realized that I need to take time to process things and this in no way reflects my intelligence.

DEEP INTO THE DETAILS OF SPACE EXPLORATION

I work for the Federal Aviation Administration (FAA) as an aerospace engineer in the Office of Commercial Space Transportation. Our office licenses private companies that want to launch within the U.S. and abroad if they're a U.S. company. We license companies like SpaceX, Blue Origin and other rocket companies that want to send satellites or other payloads into space (for some, eventually tourists). It's an exciting industry and our goal is to facilitate and promote commercial space launches and reentries by the private sector, but most importantly, to protect the public health and safety—safety of property, national security and foreign policy interests of the U.S.

Our process is very detailed and usually begins with a company coming to us with an idea for a launch vehicle or a launch site. We then go through a process where they document their goal, trajectories, systems, hardware and avionics, how they intend to comply with our regulations and, most important of all, how they intend to mitigate risk to the public. We look at every launch vehicle system you can think of, including electrical, propulsion, thermal and guidance navigation—everything— and how those systems work together, if one affects the other, what happens if one fails and how they reduce the risk of this happening. There are a lot of time-consuming discussions, both internally and with the operator.

When a company is ready to start prepping its application, we assign a team to coordinate different portions of the process, such as airspace, so that when a rocket is launching, there are no airplanes flying in the area. We also have a lengthy environmental process where we make sure that nothing about the vehicle (such as the propellant or material onboard) is hazardous and won't affect or damage any ecosystem, habitats, surrounding environment, wildlife or any endangered species. Once they submit an application, they provide a substantial number of documents on their systems and flight safety analysis because they have to ensure that their operations are safe for where they're launching, where they're landing and if it affects populations in the vicinity.

As an aerospace engineer, I function as a project manager for all those aspects. I start the process and our team members are individual subject matter experts. I walk the team and the applicant through the process to ensure that we have a complete application and can start going through it, requirement by requirement, to make sure that they are in compliance, eventually making a determination on whether the operator should be licensed.

There's a lot that goes into a license application and it's a lengthy process, too. It's not, "Hey! I want to launch next week. Here's all our information." It can be frustrating for operators, but it's also a great time in the industry because previously the aerospace industry was limited to government launches only. The dream to go into space is now being made possible for the everyday American.

I've been doing this for eight years now and I love the front-line perspective—the excitement, the variety and the new opportunities that make this such a booming industry. From mining asteroids to manufacturing in space, there is no end. There is even talk about populating Mars. My dad has excitedly said he would like to sign up for it, to which I kindly replied, "Let a few people go and come back first!"

I will note that an aerospace engineer is not limited to what I specifically do. As an aerospace engineer, your work could focus more on aircraft for the everyday flying public, designing or fixing airplane engines or building missiles for the military, among other things. I encourage you to explore these possibilities to see if any of these pique your interest.

CHASING DREAMS FOR MORE THAN MYSELF

I'm close to both of my grandmothers and talk to them often. I've asked them, "What were your dreams when you were growing up?" The one thing both wanted to do—more than get married and start a family—was get an education. They didn't and to me, that means they had dreams outside of the conventional that were left unfulfilled. They probably would've explored different career options if they had the chance and while women don't experience the same pressures today, we don't always pursue opportunities when they are unfamiliar to us.

My career is important to me because of all the opportunities these women before me didn't have. They never even imagined that they could be so independent, own property, drive a vehicle, or vote—all things that at some point were prohibited for women. It gives me an appreciation for where I am compared to where my mother was when she was my age and the personal sacrifices that she made to push her family forward. In a way, I think the women in my family are able to experience their dreams through me and I don't take that for granted.

I've grown so much because of my career. I've been able to develop the ability to be completely neutral to everyone's input. I'm not so quick to judge because people communicate differently, and I don't know the background and influences that a person has had to make them a certain way. I've also learned that no one will ever live the same life we have lived, no matter how similar our backgrounds are. There's always something that's going to mold us or shape us differently and I think a lot of misunderstandings in life come from not seeing another person's perspective.

As a Latina in aviation, I've learned to communicate effectively. Being surrounded by extremely intelligent professionals who like to problem solve, I have been challenged in many growth-inducing ways. As you grow in your career, your expertise gives you a seat at the table and the chance to have an impact on the industry. My input is valued and I think that's amazing.

Perhaps, even more, being a Latina in aviation means we represent those that came before us. And those that come after us. You often meet people in the industry who may have a predetermined view of you because you don't fit into their mold of what a Hispanic is. This is not a limitation, but a teaching opportunity to showcase that Latinas have the potential to be impactful, and I think that's the key.

While our Latino culture is amazing in so many aspects, there are still a lot of perceived limitations on what a woman should be prioritizing. Interacting with different backgrounds has encouraged me to question many of our cultural norms. I was raised to be extremely obedient and growing up it didn't matter what I thought. If an authority figure disregarded my thoughts, feelings or sense of right and wrong, I, too, did the same. One of my biggest lessons has been to understand that a lot of times, I already have the answer and that my inner compass is just as valid.

YOU CONTROL YOUR FUTURE

As I thought about what advice to offer you and what my most important achievements have been, I looked outside my career. I discovered that those things I am most proud of are intangibles, the things I've learned about myself while I worked to achieve a work-life balance that is fulfilling. I have realized that what I perceived my flaws to be are instead my biggest strengths. You will discover your own self-truths along your journey.

As you look to your own future it's okay to blaze trails, but it's also okay not to know the path to take. When I was in college and I didn't know what I wanted to study, I tried one thing and then I ended up in another—and that's okay. Life has a funny way of showing itself to you and showing you opportunities that are excellent for you. When that happens, be sure to give value to your own opinion.

Also, remember that you are not what you do—what you do is a tool for you to grow and experience life. Through my career, I have developed the emotional intelligence to handle family situations in ways I wouldn't have 10 years ago. I know how to handle different triggers and de-escalate situations. The best thing about this is that those around you also learn from you. Life does develop in front of you as you go. If you're driving from D.C. to L.A., you don't need all the directions at once. All you need are the next 400 feet and then the next 400 feet after that, and so on. I think that applies to our everyday life, too. When we're thinking about the future, we don't need to know the nitty-gritty details of the dreams we have. Each experience is the steppingstone to the next one and with each step comes a little more clarity than before. You eventually get a pretty clear picture.

It probably sounds cliché to say that anything is possible, but it really is. We are what we think and what we eat. We have the ultimate say in how our life goes. If we're unhappy with something, we can change it. Happiness truly is a decision that we make, so I encourage you take steps toward your goals and your happiness and the road will develop ahead of you.

Karen Perez is an aerospace engineer in the Office of Commercial Space Transportation at the Federal Aviation Administration. She can be contacted at karen.perez@faa.gov.

ALL IT TAKES IS A MOMENT

BRENDA GARCIA

FAVORITE AIRCRAFT

Icon A5

FAVORITE QUOTE

"A journey of a thousand miles must begin with a single step."
—Chinese Proverb

FUN FACT

I have seen Walt Disney World's fireworks show from the sky in
an airplane!

You never know when one single choice you make will change your life. You may not be able to point at it and say, "That's it! That's when my life changed!"

I can, though, and it all goes back to the calculus test I didn't study for.

It was my junior year of high school. I was a good student, but there were times when I didn't feel like studying. This day was one of them.

Luckily for me, the career center at my school allowed a few days each year where you would be able to leave campus to attend events that aligned with your career path. Your counselor would give you a permission slip to leave school and you would make up your schoolwork later.

My best friend's dad was speaking at an aviation expo for American Airlines, and I said, "Let's go to that." She wasn't into aviation, but I wanted to go so I could miss the calculus test. We got permission and went. Of course, she thought it was boring and wanted to go home.

I said, "No, this is the coolest thing ever!" My first experience in aviation was the biggest, most grand experience. Everything and everyone that could have possibly been there was.

TAKING THE NEXT STEPS

I went home that day and said, "Mom, I want to start taking flight lessons." She was pretty surprised and asked a lot of questions, trying to figure out where this sudden interest came from.

Until then, I had been unsure about what I wanted to choose for a career. As a kid, I wanted to be a teacher, so I didn't have to work in the summer. I had also considered becoming a lawyer, but was struck with doubts. I was a good student, but I didn't know if I was good enough to do that. Then, my next-door neighbor's mom was a pharmacist. I looked up to her and thought she was pretty cool. I wondered if maybe that should be my career path.

However, after that day at the aviation expo, I knew exactly what I wanted to do. There was no question in my mind. I was going to be a pilot. From that point on, I put everything I had into working toward my goal of being a pilot. And here I am.

A TALE OF TWO JOBS

I started my career as a certified flight instructor at a flight school last July. At the time, the school was relatively small, with two instructors. When I joined, they were so glad to see me that they quit, leaving me with 15 students and teaching 15 hours a day, every day in the blink of an eye.

It's a 141 school, like a college class where you're at school and you know exactly what's coming next. Some flight schools just teach enough skills for students to get their license. We have a classroom, computers, a whiteboard and five airplanes; so it's a big, small flight school.

Flight schools such as ours require 35 hours of ground instruction in addition to 35 hours in the air. I'm a full-time instructor with a wide-open schedule, so students can book me throughout the day, a week or a month in advance. I have some students that come once a month, others that come once a day and some that come twice a week.

Lessons are broken down into two-hour segments. We go through a 20-minute pre-brief where we talk about what we're doing that day, my expectations and if they have any questions or concerns. Then we typically fly for about an hour to an hour-and-a-half session so the student can learn whatever skill I'm teaching that day, whether it's a maneuver, taxiing, take off, landing or an emergency procedure. We focus on that item for the day and then come back, sit down, talk about the experience, and I sign their logbook.

Although I didn't expect it, my second job stemmed from my first job. One of my first students got his private pilot's license and was in the market to buy an airplane. I helped him with the search and he purchased a corporate configured Bonanza aircraft—a single-engine airplane that seats five people where the seats in the back face each other. It's a small plane intended to take two or three people on a business trip.

When he bought the plane, he said, "Well, you're my pilot now." It's a nice plane and I was excited to add that to my list. I took that and ran with it—my title is chief pilot for the aviation department of Shine Transportation. On a practical level, I split my time about half and half between flight instructor and chief pilot.

Shine Transportation hauls products from fuel to food, but the reason that the owner became interested in buying an airplane is because, as he explained, "I have a transportation company and this has opened up a whole new world of things that we can transport and how fast we can transport them."

It has made a difference already. Someone went to pick up a new truck for their fleet but forgot the keys. Instead of driving back and forth to get them, my job was to fly the key to one of their other hubs and come back. It turned a mistake that would have cost a lot in fuel, time and effort into a simple, "Can you fly this up there for the company?"

I also haul parts and people. My first trip was hauling 300 pounds in parts that had to get replaced on one of their trucks that was configured for jet fuel. There was a big air show in Ocean City and they were hauling the fuel for that air show. One of the parts on the truck broke, so they loaded it into the back and I flew down to Lynchburg. They were able to get the repair done and haul the fuel that same night.

VARIETY AND RESULTS FOR THE WIN

Growing up, I knew from the time I was five years old that I would not make it in the workforce if I had to sit at a desk all day. Even within aviation, some jobs don't ring the bell for me. I had a six-week internship within the FAA. You'd think I'd love it, but it was the most miserable time of my life. I came home and cried, saying, "I can't go back tomorrow. I can't sit in front of a computer and read another 80-page document to make sure that numbers match." That solidified that I didn't want to work at a desk.

The best thing about my jobs is that no two days are the same. Even if I have the same three students for flight instructing, they aren't doing the same lesson they did the day before. If I have to make the same trip, it might be to the same location, but it's rarely for the same thing.

I'm on a continuous path of education where I take students from zero flight experience to getting their private pilot's license or whatever license they're working on. I'm a person who likes to see results. It's been rewarding that during the last year, I have helped 10 people go from absolutely no flight experience to being a private pilot and about 25 others do their first solo.

I believe that being in aviation requires discipline. You can have no skills, yet you can learn it if you practice. There is science behind it, obviously in aerodynamics, weather and other things, but I wholeheartedly believe that you don't have to be smart to be a pilot. It just requires a lot of consistent, hard work.

Learning to be a pilot is not something where you can work hard for a month, take a break and come back again for another month. If you don't use it, you lose it, is a big saying in aviation. It's not unusual for students to take three or four lessons a week for two or three weeks straight. And then they think, I've been working so hard, I deserve a break. Then they come back a few weeks later and have to repeat five of those lessons. It involves a lot of muscle memory and getting used to doing it, but it doesn't require smarts.

The biggest thing that I learned was to work hard and efficiently throughout my entire aviation career. Not just in my professional career, but college as well, where I learned to fly and earned a degree in aeronautical science.

At Embry-Riddle Aeronautical University, the flight department is structured so that you had flight lessons every other day, three hours a day. People always told me, "I can't believe you already finished your first license. You're so lucky!" which would drive me insane. I always responded with it's not luck—it's hard work and dedication.

Instead of three days a week, I asked my instructor if they were available five days a week. And on the two days I had available on the weekend, I was in the lab working on simulators. Looking back, I quickly learned that the harder you work, the easier it comes.

I always tell my students that if they see someone else that got their license and they started at the same time as you, understand that most times it's not luck; it's hard work. That also applies to being a flight instructor and chief pilot. Things don't just fall into your lap. Most of the time, it's about how much work you put in.

BE THE UNEXPECTED

As a Latina in aviation, I don't think I've been discriminated against, but I do manage to surprise people. When I walk in with a key and ask to pay the landing or ramp fee, they always say some version of, "Whoa, I was not expecting you to be the pilot."

I always think of the reasons for this as the Big 3. Are they confused that I'm a girl, that I'm petite at 5'1" on a good day, or because I'm 23? Most people in the aviation industry are 40- to 50-year-old middle-aged men. So, me being a small, brown female—they look at me and think, are you supposed to be here?

One milestone that was important to me, I was able to share with my parents—taking them on a flight to breakfast and ticking over from 999 to 1,000 flight hours, the number I needed to reach my airline transport pilot license, the golden ticket of licenses. They are my biggest support system, and I wouldn't be where I am today without them. That's why it was so important to share such a special moment together.

If you are thinking about becoming a pilot, remember, if I can do it, anybody can do it. I'm not necessarily great at anything, but I'm good at many things. You just have to work hard. Also important is understanding that people are always willing to help. You just need to find the right people and the right mentor.

For me, that's my boss at Shine Transportation. He's always pushing me, saying, "You need to do something else, go out and learn more, go out and learn a different type of airplane." He doesn't want me to get comfortable because he thinks that if you're learning, you're growing, and you should always be growing.

You don't have to follow in anyone else's footsteps. You can be the first person to venture out and try something new. It might be a jump off the deep end into a whole new world, a new career, a new everything, but I wouldn't be where I am if I didn't make the jump. Try it and see where it takes you.

Brendy Garcia is a chief pilot for Shine Transportation and flight instructor at a local flight school. She can be reached at GARCIB17@ my.erau.edu.

A QUIET CHILDHOOD DREAM LEADS TO A DREAM CAREER

LUZ BEATTIE

FAVORITE AIRCRAFT

Grumman HU16 Albatross

FAVORITE QUOTE

You can't teach anyone who knows it all.

FUN FACT

Coincidentally, I share a birthday with Amelia Earhart.

I've always wanted to fly. I don't know how as a child I got that idea in my head. Maybe it was a dream, since I was not exposed to aviation. All I knew was that I wanted to fly. Growing up in a South American country in the 1960's didn't provide much opportunity to dream that a woman could achieve a career in a male-dominated field and aviation was out of the question.

Yet, while I was growing up, my favorite show was "The Flying Nun." It certainly wasn't because I wanted to be a nun, but it was definitely because there was a woman who could fly. It was a deep-seated desire that it seemed I could never achieve. At that stage of my life, it never occurred to me that I could fly for a living, but it was always there.

Like thousands of other children, I was fortunate that my parents had the courage to immigrate to the United States in the 1970s. It wasn't easy for us. In my formative years, I was navigating a new life, in a new country, with a new culture and language. It was overwhelming, but at the same time, I remembered that early dream that I wanted to fly.

So, how could I do that? From my perspective, the best way to fly was to join the military, but I had no interest in entering the military and I completely dismissed the idea. Did I have other options?

While in my senior year of high school, I was offered an internship at a major bank in New York. I was growing up on Staten Island, New York, and that was the typical pattern for my new peers and me—go to college for business while working at a major bank in downtown Manhattan, take the ferry every morning, punch the clock and take the ferry home at night. Everybody did it. I did it, too, but I knew there was always something more that I wanted.

I took the 7 o'clock ferry every morning. I hung out with my friends. I even met my future husband when a freighter crashed into the Staten Island Ferry in 1981. While attending school at night, I got my associate degree in Business from St. John's University. I fit into the perfect "cog-in-the-machine" mentality. Everyone was doing it. It seemed so natural, yet there was something I was missing.

I'm not saying it was fate, but while visiting a bookshop at lunch during my fledgling business career, there was an aviation magazine on the rack. I began casually thumbing through it and saw that it featured aviation colleges. That was it. A lightbulb went off. Why couldn't I do this? Why should I be pigeonholed into the common expectations of my surroundings? Why couldn't I achieve my dreams?

As luck would have it—and luck is always one of those things that play such an important role in momentous events—one of the schools was Dowling College on Long Island, New York. In the same town where my now-husband grew up, where my in-laws still lived—and they offered an aeronautics and management degree. I started thinking that maybe this could be fate.

My husband and I spoke about it, and, with his encouragement, we decided that this would be the perfect time to start chasing my dream. Why not? My husband had a good job, and I could enroll at Dowling College to get my degree and enroll in their flight program. As it turned out, we couldn't finance the degree and flight program, so the plan changed. I would get my degree and then start flying.

About six months later, I figured we could probably pay for flight lessons on our own, so I found a place in Caldwell, New Jersey. I stayed with my in-laws Monday through Thursday, then commuted home and took flight lessons on the weekends. It wasn't easy, but we made it a family effort, with my husband filming my take-offs and landings on a bulky VHS camcorder. It started to occur to me that my dream could become a reality.

TAKE ADVANTAGE OF OPPORTUNITIES

Let's talk about opportunities. They are out there. They might not be obvious, but you have to have a keen eye for them. You have to be able to recognize them and then you need to capitalize on them.

Let me be clear. It was hard work, but it was fun. Nothing worth achieving is easy, but doing it while attaining your dream is fun. In the aviation field, I've worked in customer service, ticketing, as a gate agent, dealt with irate taxi dispatchers and cabbies, chased geese on the midnight shift on the tarmac of Newark Airport, as a cockpit crew scheduler for a major airline, and as a dispatcher for a helicopter outfit on the Hudson River.

After graduating from college and attaining my private pilot's license, I learned of an opportunity to become an office manager at a national flight school. The job was exciting, but I wanted to earn a career on the flight deck, so how was I going to do that? As it turned out, the flight school had a program where I could earn my instrument, commercial, CFI and CFII rating while working for them. It certainly wasn't easy (by that time, my husband and I were raising a young son), but I persevered, attained all those certificates and ratings, and started instructing at that same flight school.

As most of you probably know, those economics just don't work. It is hard to earn a living as a flight instructor in someone else's plane, so my husband said, "Why don't you just do this on your own?"

Surprised, I said, "What do you mean? Buy a plane?"

He said yes and asked me, "What is the worst that could happen?" If it didn't work out, I would just sell the plane.

He was right and I ended up buying a little Cessna 150. I had the plane and my own business for over 10 years. I have to say, I was unbelievably busy and it's one of the accomplishments I'm most proud of. Along the way, I worked with a high school program and received a couple of scholarships through the 99s and Women in Aviation that helped me get my multi-engine and multi-engine instructor rating.

Remember when I said that you should have a keen eye for opportunities? While establishing my "boutique" flight instruction business, I met many people "on the field." One of them was an experienced flight instructor, who became a mentor and good friend, who wanted to teach in my operation. He also did some part-time work as a co-pilot flying a Cheyenne for a corporation on the same field. This led to me getting multi-engine experience. I eventually became a full-time pilot for that company, flew various aircraft and then had a brief stint with a commuter airline flying CRJs.

MY DREAM JOB IN MY DREAM CAREER

All this has led me to what I consider to be my "dream job." As a member of the Aircraft Owners and Pilots Association (AOPA), I was on their website and saw a job opening for a corporate pilot. I quickly applied and was fortunate to win that job. It wasn't easy. I had to relocate to a new city, but I couldn't be happier in this new challenge. Things like that kept happening and I couldn't help but think that the stars kept aligning just for me.

Today, I still work for AOPA as the director of flight operations and their corporate pilot. They're based in Frederick, Maryland, and I've been with them for almost 12 years. I maintain stringent safety standards as a pilot as well as manage and plan the budget for the corporate aircraft. Since I'm still a flight instructor, I help colleagues reach their dream of becoming a pilot. It's a multifaceted association. I'm fortunate to have met a wide variety of pilots and have seen and flown a wide variety of aircraft. I've even been able to add my seaplane rating, tailwheel endorsement and taken some helicopter lessons.

One of the things I love the most is that there aren't two days alike. As a pilot for AOPA, I fly an average of 300 hours a year. I also love the independence, full responsibility and decision-making that come with the job. Working for AOPA offers me exposure to all the different facets of aviation that I love—going to other places, challenging airport environments and missions, such as hurricane relief, humanitarian missions, Special Olympics and Angel flights, as well as participating in the Air Race Classic.

Being a Latina has also opened up opportunities. Being bilingual helped me to be selected to fly on some of the trips—especially those to Cuba, Mexico, and Colombia. My Latina heritage has made a difference as I travel for work, especially at many of our events. I enjoy the camaraderie with the Spanish-speaking aviation community and hearing what and where they fly.

WHEN YOU LOVE WHAT YOU DO

When you find something that you love to do, it doesn't feel like a job. To me, that's a success; I don't know how many people can say that. It has allowed me to go places I never would have, personally and professionally.

Aviation has been a significant factor in building my self-confidence. Growing up, I was shy, but the responsibility of flying gave me the confidence to ask questions and assert myself when I needed to. As a flight instructor, watching my students go through this process, it is gratifying to see the same confidence build.

I'm fortunate to have been able to fly to Cuba in a Caravan, which was exciting. I've also flown to Mexico a few times and to Colombia, where I'm from. I had the opportunity to ferry a jet to Bogota, which was particularly special because I still have family there that I hadn't seen in 20 years and I was flying a jet into the place where my dream to fly began.

SET GOALS, GRAB OPPORTUNITIES, GROW

As you follow your dreams and come upon challenges, I encourage you to persevere. When you persevere, more opportunities will come your way. You will keep reaching your goals and you won't stagnate. Stagnation, especially in aviation, is the worst thing that can happen. In aviation, you should never stop learning. Back to my favorite quote, keep an open mind. There is always so much to learn in aviation. Don't close your mind thinking you already know something.

When you reach one goal, then you should be setting another. Keep in mind that opportunities don't just land in your lap. You have to seek them out. As a young woman, a young Latina, don't be afraid to ask for help or to ask for advice. If you see somebody that's doing something you might want to do, talk to them. Most people want to talk about their work and you might find a great mentor.

For me, aviation has been more than a career. It's been an integral part of my life—woven throughout the years, the memories, the relationships and the dreams. When I talk to working friends, I always hear, *I've got another five years and then I'll retire. I'll finally get a chance to do this or that.* I feel like, why would I retire? It's given me a lifetime of experiences and more are ahead of me. I want to continue the dream for as long as I can.

AVIATION IS A JOURNEY

Every flight is a journey. You plan where you're going, look at the weather conditions en route and figure out the fuel and stops you'll need to reach your destination. When you take off, there could be factors that might affect your initial flight plan and as you deal with those factors, you might need to modify your plan. An aviation career is similar. You can plan with the best information available, but after you take off, evaluate the conditions and avail yourself of the best contingencies. Most of all, enjoy the journey.

Luz Beattie is the director of flight operations and corporate pilot for AOPA, the Aircraft Owners and Pilots Association. She can be reached at Luz.Beattie@AOPA.org.

A LATINA IN CONTROL

LOUISA OCASIO

FAVORITE AIRCRAFT

The ones that land safely.

FAVORITE QUOTE

¡Yo Soy Boricua pa' que tú lo sepas!

FUN FACT

There is a town in Virginia named Louisa.

When I was in high school, my cousin had completed his commitment with the US Marine Corps, where he was an aircraft mechanic. He was studying for his civilian FAA A&P (Airframe and Powerplant) license at my grandmother's kitchen table and I would help him. That was when I started getting interested in aviation. I'd never been exposed to aviation other than a plane ride once a year to visit Puerto Rico while we lived in New York.

As the stars seemed to align, I found a scholarship offered by the Air Traffic Control Association called Aviation in My Community. It required me to write a paper as part of the competition. I received a cash award for my submission. In writing that essay, I learned more about aviation and its impact on people and the economy. I wasn't considering aviation as a career then—I didn't think it was possible for a Latina.

DISCOVERING AVIATION

After graduating high school, I wanted to become a pediatrician and was accepted into pre-med school. I had already enrolled when I learned how many years it would take to complete medical school and how expensive it would be. My parents would not be able to afford it. My mother had sold her silver coin collection and saved every penny she earned for us to move from our grandmother's house to our own home.

This was when my cousin suggested I join the Puerto Rico Air National Guard (PRANG), which would help me pay for college. So, I joined. He also mentioned there was a Federal

Aviation Administration (FAA) building on the way to the National Guard. He said I should stop in and ask them about their co-op program, a work-study program where you go to college for one semester, and then alternate working for the FAA the following semester.

I looked up the college that had the aviation program. My cousin took me there, and when I arrived, it was the last day of registration! I ran up to the program director and explained that I needed to register, but I didn't know what to do. He kindly helped me with registration and, just like that, I was enrolled in an Aviation Bachelor of Science Program.

Shortly after, I visited the University Aviation Department and inquired about the Co-op program. I got the information I needed, returned to the Combined En Route Approach Control (CERAP) and registered for the Air Traffic Control Entry Exam. Once the date came to take the exam, my cousin dropped me off early in the morning and picked me up hours later. I passed, was accepted into the FAA co-op program and started the next semester at the San Juan CERAP.

As co-op students, we attended classroom training, monitored the control room operations and were tasked with making changes to the multiple publications and orders controllers used to do their job. This was before electronic copies were made available.

We would spend hours swapping pages and making pen/ink changes when we were not in training or monitoring. Though back then it seemed insignificant, I believe it helped me learn and understand the numbering of the publications and the numbers, which would later become a great skill that helped me become successful.

Being a co-op student was so much fun! I made lifelong friendships and the extra income helped me pay some college expenses. Once I completed my aviation management degree and the co-op program, I was on my way to the Mike Monroney Aeronautical Center (MMAC) in Oklahoma City for the air traffic control screen. This was the second time I had been away from home alone. I remember how scared I was, just like it was yesterday.

LEARNING ON THE JOB

Today, I work as an Air Traffic Services representative (AJT)/Air Traffic Watch Officer (AWO) for the Joint Air Traffic Operations Command (JATOC) at the FAA Air Traffic Control System Command Center (ATCSCC), which is the focal point for all National Airspace System (NAS) events. My position of record is the air traffic control tower Operations Manager at Dulles Air Traffic Control Tower (IAD). I lead a group of dedicated operations supervisors that provide first-level supervision to air traffic controllers who ensure the safe and efficient movement of airplanes.

At the ATCSCC, I gather all the data and work with other elements: tech ops, flight operations, safety, domestic events, network security and, my favorite, systems operations.

It's a collaborative effort with a lot of moving parts. My job is to encompass all information in one unified message keeping senior executives up to date with all information regarding what is happening on the NAS.

I message information necessary to help senior leadership make decisions. In a crisis event, we're the focal point and we make sure that the NAS remains stable until the executive incident manager comes on and takes charge. We also offer facilities advice or assistance in determining their operational contingency levels. It's an exciting place to be right now.

I like what I do because I learn a lot and it's never routine or boring. It's like a puzzle that you must solve. In this position, we're not just talking about only one aircraft, we're talking about the entire airspace system and how each action or inaction impacts the entire NAS. It's a domino effect.

While growing up, I didn't know something like this existed. I was the kid always playing with the little kids. When I grew up, I wanted to be a teacher or a pediatrician, but when it came time to go to college, it was unaffordable. So, I had to think of something else.

AN EXCITING CAREER IN AVIATION

Today, there are so many exciting career opportunities for Latinas in aviation. It wasn't always that way. When I started, it was a white, male-dominated career field. I hope to encourage and be a role model for others. In the last few years, I think it has changed. There is more diversity, opportunities and awareness, which is great.

Back in the day, some 30 years ago, when I was 18 or 19, there were not many women in the air traffic control career field. As a co-op student, an instructor told me I didn't belong there—girls should stay home barefoot and pregnant.

Even my uncle, who worked for an airline, said working as an air traffic controller was not a woman's job. However, after I returned from the academy as a successful air traffic controller, his level of respect for me was high. We never talked about the subject again, but if anybody was proud of me, it was my uncle.

Today, we are telling the other side of the story, where there are no limits. You could be female, male, black, white or Puerto Rican for any job. There is no race, color or gender to any career. That's important to me because I didn't have that growing up.

It means a lot for me to be able to say look, I did it. I came from poverty. We lived in a one-bedroom apartment—three girls and my parents. I used to take three buses to go to college. I didn't have a car and couldn't afford to live near the college. I had to make a lot of sacrifices.

My cousin, though, was the wind beneath my wings. I didn't appreciate it as much then, because I was just a kid, but now I realize he was the key to my success. He introduced me to aviation; he introduced me to the Air National Guard and he encouraged me. He was amazing.

There are still some challenges, but you have the same potential as anyone else. They may have privileges, but you have the same opportunities. Make sure you are ready when your opportunity comes. I am an advocate for aviation outreach, specifically for the underprivileged and minorities, because I want to ensure they know that, if they are interested, this is a career field where they can be successful.

AVIATION CHANGED MORE THAN MY LIFE

My parents encouraged us to get an education. My sisters and I were the first in our family to earn a college degree and have a profession versus an occupation. In doing that, we were able to be role models and I could give my daughter a more comfortable upbringing.

I was able to help my parents when they got older, which was essential to me because they gave us so much love and kindness. They worked hard all their life to raise three girls in on a low income. I always thought, *wow, they work long hours, take the train and walk to work.* We would walk long city blocks to save fare money. When I went to school, my mom gave me lunch money and bus fare, I would walk home to save my bus fare so I could buy myself an Icee for lunch.

Now that I'm older, I say that wasn't so bad, but I am grateful my daughter doesn't have to worry about that. When you gain the perspective of age, you have a sudden appreciation—a different appreciation—for the things that your family and your parents did for you, and how much they accomplished with so little.

One of those things my parents did was take us every year to Puerto Rico for the holidays. I remember how we walked to this travel agency and my mom put a deposit, like layaway, toward our airfare to Puerto Rico. We never missed a Three Kings Day or New Year's Eve in Puerto Rico, complete with gifts.

Aviation also changed the way I look at myself and how I interact with others. It gave me the self-confidence I needed to succeed in this field. As a Latina, I wasn't raised to be assertive, authoritative, strong or independent. I see the shift now in literature that I read and stories that I am exposed to, but for my generation it is an internal struggle because being Latina is different. The culture is different. You honor your parents and your family differently. You are raised believing there is a difference between what a woman is allowed to do vs. what a man can do.

For me, being a Latina in aviation is all about being a role model and sharing my knowledge and experiences, because challenges come with being a female and, even more so, as a Latina. As I see it, it's my opportunity to tell young women, Latinas, don't get discouraged. I've had challenges, I've been discriminated against, I've suffered micro-aggressions and I've been passed over for promotions because of the color of my skin. But I'm making it, I still have room to grow and I'm still pursuing opportunities to develop and be useful to the agency.

Many times, young people from Puerto Rico reach out to me and ask, "Can you look at my resume? Can you tell me what opportunities are available? Can you talk about your position or when you worked at this place or that place?" That's the cool part—helping others.

I think of my achievements in terms of having the opportunity to provide mentorship and advice, and to be able to say I've been there. It is very rewarding to have these individuals, these women, come to me or for someone else to tell them, "You should contact Louisa. She's an excellent mentor." Being able to give back is what I'm proudest of.

THERE ARE NO LIMITS

No matter what field you go into, whether aviation or something else, don't let anyone put limitations on you, and don't limit yourself. There will be plenty of people out there wanting to do that for you, saying you can't do that because you're a female, you're a Latina or your English is not good. I think people don't realize how offensive that is.

In the Latino community, it's very much about family, and it's challenging to find a balance between being family oriented and being a professional. I don't care what they say about work-life balance, something always has to give, which can be tricky, but you'll find that balance and still pay tribute to your heritage.

You should always be true to yourself and your culture. My daughter knows the sacrifices I've made working long shifts, missing important dates, working holidays and all that comes with this career field. It's very challenging. But there are accountants, administrative positions, doctors and engineers in the FAA, not just airplanes, pilots or controllers. Be flexible and work toward achieving whatever your heart desires. You can do anything. Don't try to be someone else; your uniqueness is what makes you special and valuable. You can still be a Latina, honor your heritage, have your values and be assertive, powerful, and successful.

Louisa Ocasio is the operations manager at Dulles Air Traffic Control Tower, an Air Traffic Services representative (AJT) / Air Traffic Watch Officer (AWO) for the Joint Air Traffic Operations Command (JATOC) at the FAA Air Traffic Control System Command Center (ATCSCC). She can be reached at LouisaOcasio@ gmail.com.

ABOUT THE AUTHORS

COLLEGE PARK AVIATION MUSEUM

College Park Aviation Museum is part of the College Park Aviation Campus and overlooks the active runway of the historic College Park Airport, the world's oldest continuously operating airport since 1909. The museum tells the remarkable story of the "Field of Firsts" where history, innovation and enterprise continue to thrive!

The College Park Aviation Museum is dedicated to preserving and promoting aviation innovations in College Park Airport and in Prince George's County. Through hands-on interactives, special exhibits, stories, artifacts, events and educational programming for children, families and adults, the museum strives to celebrate historic innovations and ignite curiosity around S.T.E.A.M.

The museum is a 27,000-square-foot, state-of-the-art facility. Visitors to the museum step into an open 1 1/2 story exhibit space, which highlights the display of unique aircraft and artifacts that share the diversity of aviation in our area.

College Park Aviation Museum is part of the Maryland National Capital Park and Planning Commission, Prince George's County Department of Parks and Recreation.

www.collegeparkaviationmuseum.com

FIELD OF FIRSTS FOUNDATION, INC.

The Field of Firsts Foundation exists to further the educational and historic preservation mission of the College Park Aviation Museum at the historic College Park Airport through fundraising and advocacy. Originally formed to raise funds for the design and construction of the museum, the Foundation today is the tax-exempt entity that allows generous donors to enhance the programing and exhibits at the museum. Funds collected through museum memberships and donations, corporate grants and sponsorships are used to help defray the costs of school field trips and other educational programs at the museum.

Established in 1909 as the military demonstration site for the Wright Brothers, College Park Airport holds the distinction as the world's oldest continually operating airport. College Park is the home of a number of aviation "Firsts," including the first mile-high flight by a powered airplane, the first controlled helicopter flight and the first female passenger. The first airmail flight operated by the U.S. Post Office Department took off from College Park Airport.

The Field of Firsts Foundation honors these historic accomplishments and continues to serve the museum and the community through our efforts.

To support us visit: www.FieldofFirsts.com.

Made in the USA
Monee, IL
28 June 2023